THE RETURN

SHAWN BOONSTRA
HENRY FEYERABEND

FOREWORD BY
MARK FINLEY

REVIEW AND HERALD® PUBLISHING ASSOCIATION
HAGERSTOWN, MD 21740

The authors assume full responsibility for the accuracy of all facts
and quotations as cited in this book.

Texts credited to NEB are from *The New English Bible*. © The
Delegates of the Oxford University Press and the Syndics of the Cambridge
University Press 1961, 1970. Reprinted by permission.

This book was
Designed by Mark O'Connor
Cover photo by PhotoDisc
Electronic makeup by Shirley M. Bolivar
Typeset: Bembo 11/12

PRINTED IN U.S.A.

06   05   04   03   02   5 4 3 2 1

R&H Cataloging Service
Boonstra, Shawn and Henry Feyerabend
    The return

    1. Antichrist.   2. Second Coming.   3. Rapture (Christian eschatol-
ogy)—Controversial literature.   I. Feyerabend, Henry.   II. Title.

236.9

ISBN 0-8280-1700-X

FOREWORD

The concepts of the secret rapture and the antichrist are topics of great interest today. Popular televangelists preach their theories on television and cable. Videos circulate their ideas everywhere. Movies dramatize the secret rapture and the rise of the antichrist with the latest Hollywood special effects. And novels based on the teaching dominate the best-seller lists. Even nonreligious people are intrigued by such speculation. But what does Scripture really teach about Christ's return and the Second Coming?

The Return, written by my It Is Written colleagues Henry Feyerabend and Shawn Boonstra, examines these widespread and popular concepts. They show the history of the secret rapture teaching and compare it with what the Bible actually teaches. Feyerabend and Boonstra convincingly demonstrate that the secret rapture is a recent theological aberration of dubious history and totally contrary to everything the Bible has to say about Christ's return. It is a Protestant version of an interpretation of prophecy developed by the Counter-Reformation to put off into the future an antichrist that already existed. To explode its errors, they examine step by step what the Bible declares about the blessed hope and the nature of the antichrist.

Reading its pages, you come away thinking, *That's simple. Why didn't I understand it sooner?*

Truth rings clear in its pages. *The Return* is thoroughly researched, meticulously documented, and powerfully illustrated. In my view, it is a must-read for any seeker after truth.

I have been richly blessed as I have perused its pages, and I know you will be too. I am sure I will be referring to its pages again and again, as will the reader.

May our Lord of all truth speak to you as you read these pages.

—Mark A. Finley
Thousand Oaks, California

CONTENTS

Chapter 1

THE RETURN

Shawn Boonstra

Check your Bible carefully. Immediately after the cruci-fixion of Christ, His disciples are nowhere to be found. A crucified criminal and a Roman centurion had the courage to declare their faith in earth's darkest hour, but the disciples appear to have evaporated into thin air. They didn't even come back for Jesus' body. Joseph of Arimathea and Nicodemus went to the government authorities to claim it. Neither did the disciples take part in planning a funeral—others had to do that. Joseph provided a tomb. Nicodemus brought embalming spices.

The disciples? They disappeared. We don't hear from them again until Sunday evening: "Then the same day at evening, being the first day of the week, when the doors were shut where the disciples were assembled for fear of the Jews" (John 20:19).

Those who were closest to Christ vanished because they were afraid. Just the previous week, their expectations had soared. Their Master had entered the city of Jerusalem the way a king might arrive, amid shouts of triumph and the waving of palm branches. People hailed Him as the conquering king who would overthrow years of Roman oppression. The disciples dreamed of high-ranking government posts.

It's amazing what a difference just one day can make. The authorities arrested Jesus on Thursday night. An illegal court forced a conviction before daybreak. By sundown Friday, Jesus was dead—and so were the disciples' hopes. The kingdom they'd dreamed about and thought Jesus had announced would be no more. They went into hiding, certain that they would be the next ones to hang on a cross.

It was devastating to the disciples—more devastating than any military coup in history has ever been to an overthrown government, because it wasn't an earthly kingdom that they had lost. It was the kingdom of God. All was lost—or so they thought. Perhaps two hikers on the road to Emmaus best summed up how Jesus' followers suddenly felt: "But we trusted that it had been he which should have redeemed Israel" (Luke 24:21).

Downcast. Defeated. Despondent. Disconsolate. They felt it must surely have been the worst moment in the history of God's people. Then something happened that changed their minds—and the course of world history: "Then the same day at evening, being the first day of the week, when the doors were shut where the disciples were assembled for fear of the Jews, came Jesus and stood in the midst, and saith unto them, Peace be unto you. And when he had so said, he shewed unto them his hands and his side. Then were the disciples glad, when they saw the Lord" (John 20:19, 20).

This passage of Scripture represents one of the single most important defining moments in human history. We find more wrapped up into a few words than we would dare to comprehend. "Then were the disciples glad, when they saw the Lord."

The Bible teaches that when Jesus returns, we will all be changed in a moment (1 Corinthians 15:52). That Sunday night the disciples were changed in a moment. One look at the risen Jesus banished their fears forever. After this single defining moment we never again see the disciples hiding like cowards.

Prior to the Crucifixion, Peter seemed mostly interested in saving his own skin. He denied knowing Jesus in order to avoid hanging on a cross beside Him. After the Resurrection, however, the disciple's interests shifted dramatically. Going from protecting himself to answering the call of Jesus and saving a lost world, he preached 3,000 people into the kingdom of God in one day. People actually *marveled* at his boldness: "Now when they saw the boldness of Peter and John, and perceived that they were unlearned and ignorant men, they marvelled; and they took knowledge of them, that they had been with Jesus" (Acts 4:13).

The Resurrection and the empty tomb of Christ are the highest authority for the Christian faith. No other religion can point to an empty tomb and a living God. The Romans who ruled in Peter's day claimed the emperor as one of their gods, yet they knew full well that emperors all finished their careers in tombs. Today the Roman Empire is dead, but Christianity still lives. In fact, about 2 billion people in the world—about one third of the world's population—claim to be Christians.

Nothing could silence disciples who had seen Jesus come back from the dead. The Resurrection and the promise of the angels that Jesus would return in glory were both Christianity's best offensive weapon and best defense against the attacks of the enemy. Beatings, scourgings, and even threats of death couldn't keep the first followers of Jesus Christ from talking about what they had seen. James the Great was beheaded (Acts 12:1, 2). James the Lesser had his head beaten in with a club.[1] Tradition declares that Philip was whipped, imprisoned, and crucified in Phrygia, Mark dragged to death in Alexandria, Thomas impaled on a spear in India, and Peter crucified upside down.

One by one Jesus' followers met with terrible deaths, and yet nothing could silence them. Why? Because not only had Jesus prophesied that He would come back from the dead, but He had also declared that He would return to earth. Nothing could stop the kingdom of heaven anymore. Nothing.

Martyrdom was of little consequence. When Jesus came back (and He surely would) He would set everything straight. And He would arrive with a reward—an eternity in the glorious kingdom that He would establish. Said Jesus: "Whoever shall lose his life for my sake and the gospel's, the same shall save it" (Mark 8:35).

At the end of his life Paul knew that he was going to make the supreme sacrifice for the sake of the gospel. It didn't worry him in the slightest, because he knew that the risen Jesus was going to return: "I have fought a good fight, I have finished my course, I have kept the faith: henceforth there is laid up for me a crown of righteousness, which the Lord, the righteous judge, shall give me at that day: and not to me only, but unto all them also that love his appearing" (2 Timothy 4:7, 8).

The empty tomb and the returning Savior have given Christianity a powerful appeal that nothing has been able to stop for nearly 2,000 years. Threats are useless against Christians, because they know that Jesus is coming. One day Christian graves will open, and His followers will receive their reward.

That knowledge has given Christians untold courage throughout the centuries. They have banked everything on what they have called the "blessed hope." Christians know that a God who can conquer the tomb will eventually return and overthrow all wickedness. Nothing can stop them in the work of courageously carrying the gospel to the whole earth, because they realize that when the job is finished, Jesus will return (Matthew 24:14).

Perhaps Christian courage is the reason the minions of the devil hate the Bible's teaching about Christ's return. When He came the first time, Satan succeeded in confusing a whole nation to the point that they completely misunderstood the role of the Messiah. They hoped He would be a political Messiah—but He was not. As a result, they rejected and killed God's Son. Even His own followers cowardly locked themselves in a room, trembling in fear.

It almost worked, but when Jesus appeared to His disciples and promised to come back for them, a new hope was born in their hearts. There would be no mistakes this time. The next time Jesus arrived, He would establish His kingdom of glory (Matthew 25:31).

Although not completely triumphant, Satan was remarkably successful in confusing the biblical prophecies of Jesus' first advent. The prophecies, misunderstood and misapplied, actually became a barrier to accepting the Messiah for many people. By the time Jesus returned to heaven, He had only 120 believers (Acts 1:15). That number, however, coupled with the courage that a resurrection can bring, managed to carry the gospel to the entire Roman Empire in one generation.[2]

Satan's strategy, while not prevailing completely, was nevertheless so successful that we must ask ourselves: Is it possible that he will try it again with the biblical prophecies about Christ's second coming?

The return of Jesus Christ is perhaps the most talked-about subject in the Bible. In fact, Dwight L. Moody estimated that Scripture mentions it more than 2,500 times. God knows that above all other subjects, the hope of Jesus' return gives us the courage to press forward with the commission He has given us.

If the forces of satanic darkness can confuse us on the very subject that gives us our hope, they stand a real chance of stifling the gospel work that God has given Christians to do. For example, what if Satan could convince us that the prophecies of Jesus' return were merely a metaphor for "spiritual awakening" or some other such thing? You can find Christians today who say so,[3] and more often than not, they are *not* busy proclaiming the gospel and saving lost souls.

Bible prophecy assures us that the devil knows his timetable: "Woe to the inhabiters of the earth and of the sea! for the devil is come down unto you, having great wrath, because he knoweth that he hath but a short time" (Revelation 12:12).

There's a lot at stake, as far as fallen angels are concerned. When Jesus emerged from the tomb, they knew their fate was sealed, but they still have not given up on confusing the world in a last-ditch attempt to embarrass the cause of Christ and to keep people from the gates of Paradise.

One of the most powerful places for the forces of perdition to strike is directly at the teachings of the resurrection and the return of Christ, for without them the cause of Christianity would quickly lose the momentum that gave it its powerful birth.

Has there been another attack on the teachings of Bible prophecy? Absolutely—and just as with the first one in New Testament times, it's being perpetrated by God's own people. Somebody's trying to force Christians back into a locked room to shake in their boots, because they know that we will be more than glad the next time we see the Lord. "And it shall be said in that day, Lo, this is our God; we have waited for him, and he will save us: this is the Lord; we have waited for him, we will be glad and rejoice in his salvation" (Isaiah 25:9).

---

[1] Historical accounts of the martyrdom of the apostles appear in Foxe's *Book of Martyrs*.

[2] See Colossians 1:23, in which Paul is able to declare that the gospel had been preached to "every creature which is under heaven."

[3] Generally speaking, they're the same Christians who now deny the literal and physical resurrection of Jesus from the dead.

Chapter 2

LEFT BEHIND

Henry Feyerabend

Hundreds of people missing from an airliner, with nothing but their clothes left behind. Other planes lose flight crews.

Car pileups, chaos, planes down all over and at every major airport.

So many cabbies disappear from the cab corral at O'Hare that volunteers have to be brought in to move the cars that have been left running with the former drivers' clothes still on the seats.

Cars driven by people who spontaneously disappeared careen out of control.

A woman in labor suddenly barren as the fetus disappears.

CNN footage shows the woman going from very pregnant to nearly flat stomach.

Nurse at her side disappears, leaving the uniform, stockings, and all in a pile atop her shoes.

At a burial, three of six pallbearers stumble and drop the casket when the other three disappear. When they pick up the casket, it too is empty.

These incidents appear in a book written by best-selling authors Tim LaHaye and Jerry B. Jenkins.

Entertainment Weekly describes the work as: "Christian thriller. Prophecy-based fiction. Juiced-up morality tale. Call it what you like, the *Left Behind* series . . . now has a label its creators could never have predicted: blockbuster success" (*Left Behind* [Wheaton, Ill.: Tyndale House Publilshers, Inc., 1995], quoted on flyleaf).

Such ideas are not new to me. As a boy I had my first encounter with the scenario described in this work. Nothing unusual ever seemed to happen in the little prairie town of Waldheim, Saskatchewan, where I grew up. So the occasional entertainment in the town hall always had a good attendance.

"Tonight we're going to see a movie that talks," one of my close friends reminded me. We had seen slides and silent movies, but a sound motion picture was a real novelty for young country boys.

We got there early in order to get a good seat, but the hall was already full. At first the projector with its big reels was the center of attention. The whirring of the machine seemed to compete with the crackling sound of the loudspeaker. But soon everyone's fascination shifted to the picture on the screen. The title of the film was *The Missing Christians*.

As the plot developed, we became acquainted with its principal characters: a family in which the wife and some of the children were Christians, but the husband had never committed his life to Christ.

And then the rapture! To the background of music by a male quartet singing "We Shall Rise," eerie white souls winged their way to heaven during the night.

"Where is my wife and family?" the husband asked the next morning. He looked through the house, but she and the children were gone. He called his neighbors, but they couldn't help him. Family members were missing in their homes as well. When he tried to phone the police, the telephone lines were jammed. Everywhere people were missing. The afternoon headlines announced the strange disappearance of millions of people from the earth. Confusion and consternation spread around the world.

The next day at school everyone was talking about the film—and the coming rapture. Some of my friends discussed the subject as I walked into the room. "Where does the Bible describe this event?" I asked.

They gasped as they gazed at me in total shock. "Don't you even believe the Bible? Didn't you pay attention to the film last night?"

I discovered that it was sacrilegious to question the rapture.

Since my first encounter with the rapture concept, others have told me many times that it is the only true interpretation of Scripture. Television evangelists routinely expound it as a basis for their fundamentalist teaching. Bible schools, training ministers for the pulpits of the land, teach the dispensational approach to Bible study. One preacher said: "This key was made for this lock" (Henry C. Thiessen, "Will the Church Pass Through the Tribulation?" p. 17).

The *Scofield Study Bible* assures us that "there can be no adequate understanding of rightly dividing the Word of God, except from a standpoint of dispensation truth" (Philip Mauro, *The Gospel of the Kingdom,* p. 6).

Henry Thiessen says: "The evidence is cumulative. . . . When all the facts are taken together, there can be no doubt that this is the teaching of Scripture" (Thiessen, p. 17).

C. A. Mackintosh states boldly that not to accept the rapture teaching is to overlook "the plainest teaching of Scripture" (C. G. McGavern, *Rapture or Resurrection?* p. 37).

John Darby, one of the founders of the rapture theory, considered anyone who did not agree with him to be in "unmingled darkness," showing the "absence of spiritual intelligence." Speaking of the opposition to his theories, he referred to the "utter futility of its reasonings." He considered opposing views as a "mass of unscriptural fancies and follies" (David MacPherson, *The Great Rapture Hoax,* p. 177).

Darby visited Dwight L. Moody's church in Chicago a number of times, but the two men disagreed on the topic. In reaction, Darby said that "Moodyism and the United States religion is a most deadening and worldly-making principle" (*ibid.,* p. 176).

Many dispensationalists equate not believing in a secret rapture with not accepting the Bible. One former dispensationalist writes: "Even today, some of my dearest friends are convinced that I have departed from the evangelical faith" (Clarence B.

Bass, *Backgrounds to Dispensationalism,* Vol. I, p. 9).

Some observers have considered dispenationalism to be the lifeblood of the electronic church. They have called it the "glue that holds the many factions of fundamentalism together."

For years I have searched the Scriptures looking for the illusive reference to the pretribulation rapture so widely taught and believed in. I have asked everyone I could talk to for help in finding the particular Bible prophecy that inspired the film.

Someone told me to look at Matthew 24:40, 41. I read: "Then shall two be in the field; the one shall be taken, and the other left. Two women shall be grinding at the mill; the one shall be taken, and the other left." But looking at the context of this verse, I quickly discovered that it was not speaking of a secret appearance of our Lord. Verse 30 of the same chapter sets the stage for what follows, describing His coming in these words: "And then shall appear the sign of the Son of man in heaven: and then shall all the tribes of the earth mourn, and they shall see the Son of man coming in the clouds of heaven with power and great glory."

It seems evident that this verse describes the same event recorded in the book of Revelation: "Behold, he cometh with clouds; and every eye shall see him" (Revelation 1:7).

We find no indication of a *secret* rapture in which those left behind find piles of clothing and wonder where the people have disappeared. Instead, Scripture depicts Christ as coming in clouds with power and great glory.

Matthew 24:27 announces: "For as the lightning cometh out of the east, and shineth even unto the west; so shall also the coming of the Son of man be." Lightning is not something easily hidden. The fact that Matthew 24 does not refer to the rapture will not come as a surprise to informed believers in a pretribulation rapture. As a result, they seek to explain it away. Both John Darby, one of the founders of this theory, and John Walvoord, a modern authority in the field, clearly affirm that Christ's Olivet discourse on the end of the age does not address the church and has nothing to do with the rapture.

Darby said: "I still believe that Matthew 24, at least to verse thirty-one, is addressed to the disciples as Jews. . . . I do not think it was addressed to the church" (W. Kelly, ed., *The Collected Writings of J. N. Darby,* Vol. IV, p. 4).

Walvoord writes: "It is important to bear in mind, in the study of Matthew 24 and 25, that the rapture is not mentioned in these chapters. . . . The rapture isn't found anywhere in Matthew, Mark, or Luke (or in any part of the Olivet Discourse)" (John Walvoord, "Christ's Olivet Discourse on the End of the Age," *Bibliotheca Sacra* CXXVIII [1971]: 114).

With the Gospels placed out of bounds by dispensationalist scholars themselves, where do we find the basis for the claim that the *Left Behind* books and movie are based on biblical prophecy? Where do we find the rapture mentioned in the Bible?

As I continued my search, some claimed to find the rapture in the writings of Paul, especially 1 Thessalonians 4:16: "For the Lord himself shall descend from heaven with a shout, with the voice of the archangel, and with the trump of God: and the dead in Christ shall rise first."

Somehow, some elements of this verse are missing in the *Left Behind* description of the rapture. Had they been included, the story would lose its luster. Had the Lord come with a shout, surely those left behind would have heard it. Advocates of the secret rapture fail to mention anyone hearing the voice of the archangel and the sound of God's trumpet. A trumpet depicts a public announcement, never something furtive or secret.

Though proponents of the rapture theory tell us explicitly that the event described by Paul takes place seven years before the event described in Matthew 24, the two events sound strangely similar: "And he shall send his angels with a great sound of a trumpet, and they shall gather together his elect from the four winds, from one end of heaven to the other" (Matthew 24:31).

Notice the elements of striking similarity. Both passages refer to:

- The coming of Christ
- The sounding of a trumpet
- The accompanying presence of angels.

The natural conclusion of Bible scholars throughout the centuries has been that the rapture of the church and the resurrection of the dead in Christ will take place at His glorious appearing.

Those who believe in a secret rapture conclude that Christ's second coming has two aspects—(a) the rapture, followed by (b) His second coming in glory and majesty. DeHaan claimed that most Christians are confused because they fail to distinguish between the rapture and the revelation of Christ at His second coming (M. R. DeHaan, *The Second Coming of Jesus*, p. 41). As he explains the sequence, at the "rapture" Jesus comes *for His saints*. Then at the "revelation" He comes *with His saints*. He bases his reasoning on three words used for His coming.

"Three words are used in connection with the second coming of Christ. These three words are: *Parousia*, *Apokalypsis*, and *Epiphenia*. The first two are most commonly used when speaking of the Lord's return. The Parousia refers generally to a period of time ushered in by the return of the Lord for His Church—a time followed by the Tribulation period. . . . The word *Parousia* literally means 'presence.' At His descent in the air He will come to take us into His presence" (*ibid.*, p. 42).

This may sound very impressive to those who do not know biblical Greek. However, a careful analysis of the use of these three words does not support the dispensationalist view. Different scholars have made many studies, and one outstanding investigation has been conducted by Allis, an acknowledged authority in the field of linguistics. (Loraine Boettner, in *The Millennium* [pp. 163, 164], summarizes the results of Allis's research.)

The apostle Paul uses the word *parousia* 14 times, and eight times he is referring to the glorious appearing of Christ. Thessalonians uses it for the catching up of the believers. But to say that it *always* refers to the rapture spells trouble for dispensationalists. In one reference it speaks of the coming of our Lord Jesus Christ *with all His saints* (1 Thessalonians 3:13). Another reference employs it in connection with the slaying of antichrist. In this same passage Paul uses a combination of the two words *epiphaneia* and *parousia* (2 Thessalonians 2:8). Paul's combination of the two expressions describes what apparently is one and the same event.

Paul uses the word *apokalypsis* 13 times. In one instance it clearly refers to the translation of the church (see 1 Corinthians

1:7). And in 2 Thessalonians 1:7, the reference just as clearly means the glorious appearing.

Of all the New Testament writers, only Paul employs the term *epiphaneia*. Here again, in one instance the reference to the catching up of the saints seems unmistakable (see 2 Timothy 4:1, 8). In others, the allusions to judgment and glory identify it with the glorious appearing (2 Timothy 4:1; Titus 2:13).

Dispensationalists assure us that at the rapture Christ comes *for* His saints, and at the glorious appearing He comes *with* His saints. The fact is, only one passage in the New Testament uses the expression "with all his saints"—1 Thessalonians 3:13. Jude 14 uses a similar, though slightly different, expression: "Behold, the Lord cometh with ten thousands of his saints."

If the "saints" in Jude prove a rapture, there must have been one before Sinai, because Scripture declares the saints were with God at that time. "The Lord came from Sinai, and rose up from Seir unto them; he shined forth from mount Paran, and he came with ten thousands of saints" (Deuteronomy 33:2).

Who were these saints? The book of Psalms provides the key. "The chariots of God are twenty thousand, *even thousands of angels:* the Lord is among them, *as in Sinai,* in the holy place" (Psalm 68:17).

The Lord's coming with thousands of saints refers to His arrival with thousands of angels. The word "saint" means holy one, and Scripture commonly employs it to refer to angels (see Mark 8:38).

In my lifetime search for answers on this subject, I have read every book I could find about it. I have spent many hours in great libraries well stocked with books on the subject, including that at the Moody Bible Institute. Am I alone in my bewilderment? Have I been the only person who could not find this theory in Bible prophecy?

I was in for a number of mystifying surprises.

Chapter 3

SURPRISES

Henry Feyerabend

In the previous chapter I mentioned that my research about the validity of the secret rapture doctrine brought me some surprises. Let me elaborate.

The first one that I encountered, which was rather comforting, is that I was not alone in my quest for Bible evidence.

Rowland V. Bingham, editor of *The Evangelical Christian,* looked up from the sermon he was preparing as his wife said, "I have to teach the Second Coming to my Sunday school class tomorrow morning. I've been hunting for proof of the secret rapture, but I can't seem to find it. You've preached about it often. Will you please help me find the texts?"

"Just read 1 Thessalonians 4:16," Bingham replied.

"But I *have* been reading that, and it's about the noisiest thing I can find in the Bible," she answered.

As Pastor Bingham thought about it, he realized that his answer was not satisfactory—not to his wife and her Sunday school students, and frankly not even to himself. Later he said, "In sheer desperation I took out my Bible and threw myself helplessly on the Lord."

"The weeks that followed that innocent query and the trouble into which it landed me," he reported, "is a separate story. If you hold the theory of a secret rapture of the church, try out that simple question on yourself" (in C. G. McGavern,

Rapture or Resurrection? p. 81).

Later his friend G. Campbell Morgan wrote to Mr. Bingham, saying, "I suppose I may say that across the years I have passed through very much of your own experience with regard to these prophetic matters. . . . The phrase 'secret Rapture' has to me for a long time been a very objectionable one, and utterly unwarranted in its wording, and in what it is made to stand for by the teaching of the Scripture" (George E. Ladd, *The Blessed Hope,* p. 55).

W. J. Erdman, one of the strong proponents of the rapture teaching and one of the consulting editors of the *Scofield Reference Bible,* also served as pastor of the Moody Church in Chicago. As a result of deep searching of the Scriptures he concluded that the teaching was not biblical. "Should anyone deplore the adoption of the belief that the Lord will not come any moment, as if it would take away all joy and comfort," he observed, "it is enough to answer in the words of another, 'Better the disappointment of truth than the fair but false promises of error'" (in Ladd, p. 48).

Charles R. Erdman, a scholar at Princeton University, also contributed to the Scofield Bible. "The doctrine seems to be founded upon a false interpretation of the translation, in the King James Version, of the opening verse of the second chapter of Second Thessalonians," he later decided (in Ladd, p. 51).

Other prominent defenders of the theory had similar experiences. A. J. Gordon, former pastor of Boston's Clarendon Street Baptist Church, defended the theories that have inspired the *Left Behind* novels. Later, though, he wrote a book with the Latin title *Ecce Venit* in which he rejected this entire system of interpreting Bible prophecy (Ladd, pp. 46, 47).

Henry W. Frost, a well-known preacher, after studying deeply into the matter, said that this view "might be held as truth if there were any scripture to confirm it, but (it) may not be held in view of the fact that no scripture even suggests such a process of events and many scriptures positively contradict it" (in Ladd, p. 50).

Harold J. Ockenga, a former supporter and writer on the subject, decided that "no amount of explaining can make

(1 Thessalonians 4:16, 17) a secret rapture. It is the visible accompaniment of the glorious advent of the Lord. No exegetical justification exists for the arbitrary separation of the 'coming of Christ' and the 'day of the Lord'" (in Ladd, p. 58).

Author Philip Mauro wrote: "It is mortifying to remember that I not only taught these novelties myself, but that I even enjoyed a complacent sense of superiority because thereof, and regarded with a feeling of pity and contempt those who had not received the new light" (*The Gospel of the Kingdom,* pp. 6, 7).

George Ladd tells of his college days when he strongly defended dispensationalism and the rapture theory. As a thorough student, he read widely in an attempt to find support for his beliefs. "Most of the books I read seemed to assume the whole system rather than to prove it," he found. "While many biblical passages were quoted, the exegetical problems involved appeared to me to be unsolved" (*Crucial Questions About the Kingdom,* p. 13).

Harry Ironside, a renowned Bible teacher and author of many books on the rapture, promoted the theory until his death in 1951. He often received invitations to speak on radio station WMBI, owned by the Moody Bible Institute.

R. S. Payne was a supervisor at the Moody station. After one of Ironside's broadcasts the two men had a conversation on Bible prophecy. A letter Payne wrote to Dave MacPherson tells of Ironside talking about the rapture theory, saying, "I know that the system I teach is full of holes, but I am too old and have written too many books to make any change" (MacPherson, *The Great Rapture Hoax,* p. 86).

My second surprise was the admission on the part of dispensationalist scholars that Scripture does not describe a secret rapture.

The recent past is not the first time that books on this subject have reached the best-seller status. More than 30 years ago Hal Lindsey's *The Late Great Planet Earth* went through edition after edition. Mr. Lindsey candidly said about the rapture: "It [the rapture] is not found in the Bible, so there is no need to race for your concordance, if you have one" (*The Late Great Planet Earth,* p. 137).

The *Scofield Reference Bible* militantly teaches a mystic disappearance of Christians. Yet Mr. Scofield admitted that such a belief was not something seen by the Bible prophets, but rather a new thing in the book of God—"a new promise to a new body" ("The Return of Christ in Relation to the Church," *Bibliotheca Sacra* CIX [1952]: 5).

John Walvoord writes: "The departure of the church from the earth will obviously cause quite a stir, though the Bible never seems to refer to it directly" ("Christ's Olivet Discourse on the End of the Age," p. 114).

Admittedly the Bible does not explicitly affirm the rapture theory. To find it one must follow a special method of interpretation, a point clearly stated by William K. Harrison: "The fact that *nowhere does the New Testament declare that the rapture does or does not precede the tribulation* leads to the further conclusion that the time of the rapture in relation to the great tribulation *must be inferred* from a careful analysis of those passages which are relevant" (William K. Harrison, "The Time of the Rapture as Indicated in Certain Scriptures," *Bibliotheca Sacra* CXIV [1957]: 318; italics supplied).

Amazingly, not one passage of Scripture teaches or even hints at a pretribulation rapture. C. G. McGavern, in *Rapture or Resurrection?* observes: "Let us here emphasize that it is to us a most amazing fact that there is positively not one passage of Scripture which teaches or even hints at a 'secret' coming of Christ, without the aid of much inference, interpolation, supposition, addition and deletion" (pp. 52, 53).

"Of all the religious theories," he adds, "from Pantheism to Spiritualism (with the possible exception of the Anglo-Israel heresy) this pre-tribulation, secret rapture theory is the most completely divorced from all Bible support and confirmation of any it has been our lot to encounter" (*ibid.*, p. 31).

A careful study of the history of the theory brought me face to face with some astonishing facts. None of the Church Fathers ever dreamed of the series of events by which modern preachers describe the return of Christ. The hope of the church throughout the early centuries was the visible second coming of Christ, not a pretribulation rapture.

Paul talks about the "hope of eternal life, which God, that

cannot lie, promised before the world began" (Titus 1:2). He describes that hope in the following words: "Looking for that blessed hope, and the glorious appearing of the great God and our Saviour Jesus Christ" (Titus 2:13).

The expectation of the church was the "glorious appearing," not some furtive caper in which our Lord secretly snatches His people away. He is coming in the clouds of heaven "with power and great glory" (Matthew 24:30).

If the blessed hope is in fact a pretribulation rapture, then the church has never known about it through most of its history, for the idea of a pretribulation rapture did not appear in prophetic interpretation until the nineteenth century.

Dispensationalists have pushed aside the great truths taught by our spiritual forebears. They obliterate the teachings of such great leaders as Martin Luther, Menno Simons, John Wesley, George Whitefield, Charles Spurgeon, and Dwight L. Moody. Some of the truths they taught are bastions of faith that we will need if we are to face the coming crisis predicted by the Bible.

My research on the subject of the rapture led me to some unexpected pathways. Uncovering the chain of events that planted this theory into Protestantism, it became clear that it carried a hidden agenda. It seems as if the train of logical Bible interpretation has jumped the track of sound principles and has careened into the wilderness of speculation and sensationalism. But that is not what really happened. For biblical interpretation to jump the track at all implies an accident of some sort. Rather, it was deliberately derailed.

I invite you to examine the evidence carefully.

Kenneth S. Wuest, a believer in the rapture, has well stated that unless a Bible interpretation is based on historical background, context, and an understanding of the Greek or Hebrew syntax and grammar of the original Scripture, it is only an opinion, much like untested speculation in science. "The student who follows the rules of an experiment in chemistry brings the experiment to a successful conclusion. The student who does not ends up with an explosion" ("The Rapture—Precisely When?" *Bibliotheca Sacra* CXIV, [1957]: 60).

Is the doctrine of dispensationalism a result of applying

sound Bible principles, or is it simply speculation? In pursuing its roots will we end up with an explosion that will blow the lid off one of the greatest masquerades in history?

Chapter 4

THE BIRTHDAY OF DISPENSATIONALISM

Henry Feyerabend

I t may be a bit unsettling to realize that the birthplace of the concept of a pretribulation rapture is Port Glasgow, Scotland, that the date on its birth certificate is 1830, and that a young Scottish woman originated it (see David MacPherson, *The Great Rapture Hoax,* p. 47).

David MacPherson, in his books *The Incredible Cover-up* and *The Great Rapture Hoax,* has done a great deal of research into the story of Margaret McDonald of Scotland. He asserts that the whole system of dispensational theology, as we know it today, made its debut into Protestantism through this young woman.

Miss MacDonald seems to be one of the first individuals to talk about a secret coming of Christ, thereby dividing His return into two phases. Such ideas do not appear anywhere in the writings of the church before her time.

An 1861 book, authored by Robert Norton, an Englishman who had received his M.D. when he was only 21 years old, describes her vision in the following words: "Marvelous light was shed upon Scripture, and especially on the doctrine of the second Advent, by the revived spirit of prophecy. In the following account by Miss M. M. of an evening during which the power of the Holy Gost rested upon her for several successive hours, in mingled prophecy and vision, we have an instance: *for here we first see the distinction between that final stage of the Lord's coming, when every eye shall see Him, and His prior appearing in glory to them that look for Him"* (Robert Norton, *The Restoration of Apostles and Prophets in the Catholic Apostolic Church,* p. 15 in C. G. McGavern, *Rapture or Resurrection?* p. 84; italics supplied).

MacPherson traces a direct link between Margaret MacDonald and John Darby, of the Plymouth Brethren. He says that many Christians will be shocked to "learn that Darby himself visited Margaret in her home not long after word got out that she'd succeeded in splitting the second coming atom, and he tells what he saw and heard in a little-known work of his that has been generally overlooked by historical scholars" (MacPherson, p. 67).

MacPherson also traces Darby's first acceptance of the idea of a two-phase Second Coming to 1830, the year of Margaret MacDonald's revelation. In one of his letters Darby talks about his new beliefs, commenting, "It is a remarkable circumstance, that a dear young lady, who was instrumental in setting them afloat for me . . ." (in MacPherson, p. 178).

The church that Edward Irving, another pioneer of the rapture theory, promoted featured glossolalia, or speaking in tongues, and received revelations similar to those of Margaret McDonald, possibly even by her new ideas. "Miss E. C. broke out in English in an unnatural and unaccustomed tone. . . . In the midst of this awe and reverence, I was myself seized upon by the power: and in much struggling against it, was made to cry out, and myself to give forth confession of my own sin" (in A. L. Drummond, *Edward Irving and His Circle,* pp. 186, 187).

Here is another account of what happened to Irving: "I did experience a sudden change of opinion; the passages in Matthew xxiv., two shall be in the field, one shall be taken and the other left; two women shall be grinding at the mill, the one shall be taken and the other left, were brought to me in power, accompanied with a sudden conviction I have before described" (R. Baxter, *The Narrative of Facts,* in Daniel Paynton Fuller, *The Hermeneutics of Dispensationalism,* p. 48).

S. P. Tragelles shows that the teachings of Edward Irving on the rapture rested completely upon these utterances that he attributed to the Spirit of God. "I am not aware that there was any definite teaching that there would be a secret rapture of the church at a secret coming until it was given forth as an 'utterance' in Mr. Irving's church, from what was there received as being the voice of the Spirit. It was from that supposed revelation that the modern doctrine and the modern phraseology respecting it arose. It came not from Holy Scripture, but from that which falsely pretended to be the Spirit of God, while not owning the true doctrines of our Lord's incarnation in the same flesh and blood as his brethren, but without taint of sin" (S. P. Tragelles, *The Hope of Christ's Second Coming,* in Fuller, p. 52).

Though scholars disagree as to who actually initiated the rapture theory, one thing is apparent. It did not come from Bible study, but rather it originated from some kind of revelation claiming to be the voice of the Holy Spirit.

The concept of the secret rapture made its debut into Protestantism in the early nineteenth century. MacPherson, in *The Great Rapture Hoax,* points out that Margaret MacDonald's idea of dividing the second coming of Christ into two phases, which he diagnoses as "double vision," was something completely new to Christianity. He put his thesaurus to good use when he observed: "It was fresh, novel, unique, original, authentic, firsthand, a prototype, different, unheard of, unusual, hot off the fire, untrodden, the latest scream, newborn, embryonic, newfangled, fresh as the dew, an innovation, the latest wrinkle, quite another thing, brand new, neoteric, the gloss of novelty, something else again, another order of cat, and a horse of a different color! In short, it was one of a kind" (p. 65).

But his statement is only partially correct. Margaret MacDonald's revelation was not the dawn of dispensationalism. She was 245 years too late and only introduced the concept into Protestantism. Even MacPherson observes: "If evidence should arise that someone before 1830 did the same thing, and if it could be shown that such an individual concretely influenced the development of the 1830s then, of course, my MacDonald thesis would no longer be valid" (*ibid.,* p. 121).

Margaret MacDonald was not original in her theory. It had originated 245 years before her time. As a solution to a problem, it had been carefully constructed with a hidden agenda in mind.

During the Protestant Reformation, Bible students began to emphasize the position (now known as "historicist") that the prophecies of the antichrist pointed to the medieval church. Such Bible students generally believed that the biblical terms *antichrist, the little horn, the beast, the man of sin, Babylon,* and *the harlot* all pointed to the same entity—the medieval church state, usually referred to as the Papacy. For example, Martin Luther, as an Augustinian monk in the University of Wittenberg, came reluctantly to believe that "the papacy is in truth nothing else than . . . very Antichrist" (in LeRoy E. Froom, *The Prophetic Faith of Our Fathers,* vol. 2, p. 257).

Although blunt in this assertion, Luther assured Pope Leo X on October 13, 1520, that he was not attacking him personally but "the Roman see, the Court of Rome," that Luther confessed had become "more corrupt . . . than Sodom, Gomorrha, and Babylon." Further, he added, "I have ever regretted, pious Leo, that thou shouldest now be pope when thou wert worthy of better times. The Roman See is not worthy of thee. . . . Once it was a gate of heaven; now it is the very jaw of hell. This is why I have attacked it so mercilessly" (in Froom, p. 258).

Despite his often strong language, Luther was not attacking a person or persons as such but an organization that had become corrupt because it had forsaken Christian ideals and biblical principles. Even Catholic scholars agreed, men who lived long before Martin Luther and the other Protestant Reformers. During the Middle Ages the popes behaved very badly at times. Historian Philip Schaff referred to "the shocking immoralities of the popes" that "called forth strong protests" (*History of the Christian Church,* Vol. IV, p. 290).

For instance, Arnulf, the bishop of Orleans, deplored the Roman popes as "monsters of guilt." In a council called by the king of France in 991, Arnulf indicated that the behavior of recent popes appalled him. "Looking at the actual state of the papacy, what do we behold?" he asked. Then he listed some of the sorry conditions that marked some of the recent Roman pontiffs—concupiscence, murders, cruelty, ignorance, and even illiteracy.

He reasoned that "if . . . we be bound to weigh in the balance the lives, the morals, and the attainments of the meanest [lowliest] candidate for the sacerdotal office, how much more ought we to look to the fitness of him who aspires to be the lord and master of all priests! Yet how would it fare with us, if it should happen that the man most deficient in all these virtues, one so abject as not to be worthy of the lowest place among the priesthood, should be chosen to fill the highest place of all? . . . Must he not be"—and Arnulf began quoting the Bible— "'Antichrist, sitting in the temple of God, and showing himself as God'?" (in Schaff, pp. 290, 291).

Several centuries later Eberhard II, archbishop of Salzburg (1200-1246), stated that the people of his day were quite accustomed to calling the pope "antichrist" (in Froom, vol. 1, p. 800). His comment suggests that he was but reporting what had become a fairly common opinion.

More than a century after Eberhard, when the Western church was divided between two rival popes—one in Rome and the other in Avignon, France—each pope declared that the other was the antichrist. John Wycliffe, professor of philosophy at Oxford University and translator of the Bible into English, is reputed to have regarded them both as being right: "Two halves of Antichrist, making up the perfect Man of Sin between them" (in Froom, vol. 2, p. 49).

Truly the prophetic finger pointed to the excesses of the church-state fusion during the Middle Ages. Many of the faithful were coming to recognize the reprehensible behavior of a number of the men who claimed to be head of the church. Something had to be done about it.

In the late 1500s what has come to be known as the Counter-Reformation launched an attack on the historicist approach to prophetic interpretation, seeking to divert attention away from the Papacy. Two priests especially spearheaded the movement: Spanish biblical scholar and Jesuit Francisco Ribera and Italian cardinal Robert Bellarmine. They worked hard to save face for the Roman Catholic Church, which had suffered so much at the hands of less than pious leaders. In the process the two men invented what is now known as the futurist school of interpreting biblical prophecy.

THE BIRTHDAY OF DISPENSATIONALISM

During the 1940s the monumental research of LeRoy E. Froom established the fact that this futurism, developed by Jesuits to protect the reputation of the church, was almost identical to the dispensational futurism that so many Protestants espouse today.

Prior to the work of Ribera and Bellarmine, Bible students typically interpreted the beasts and horns of biblical prophecy to be powers, not individuals. But these two influential thinkers asserted that antichrist would be revealed in the future as a malignant dictator who would establish himself in Jerusalem for three and a half literal years. They introduced a parenthesis between the time of Christ and the end of the age. At the same time they denied what is now often referred to as the year-day principle, a concept widely accepted since the time of the early church and used as a key to unlock biblical time prophecies. It taught that a "day" in biblical prophecy symbolized a literal chronological year.

Like modern futurists, Ribera applied all of the predictions found in the book of Revelation except the first few chapters to the end of time rather than to the history of the church (see G. E. Ladd, *The Blessed Hope,* pp. 37, 38).

At the same time Ribera formulated his concept of interpreting prophecy, a contemporary of his, Luis de Alcazar, another Spanish Jesuit, proposed an alternative approach. Although quite different from Ribera's way of doing prophetic interpretation, Alcazar's method achieved the same end—avoiding the identification of the medieval church-state Papacy by prophetic insight.

Alcazar said that the entities such as the little horn and the antichrist mentioned in Scripture actually referred not to a future individual but to a power in the past. He believed that the object of prophetic criticism was basically the ancient Roman Empire. Scripture, according to Alacazar's understanding, had in mind the demise of the Jewish nation, the destruction of Jerusalem, and the persecutions instituted by Roman emperors such as Nero, Domitian, and/or Diocletian. So the biblical prophecies did not extend beyond the fall of Rome in A.D. 476. This approach to biblical prophetic interpretation scholars now call "preterism."

All of this, Froom concluded, can be regarded as a deliberate plan to divert the symbols of antichrist away from the church-state Papacy. These new approaches to understanding biblical prophecy began to "confuse not a few who had stood upon the Reformation platform. Alcazar's disruptive pro-Catholic Preterist thesis was adopted into the Protestantism of the rationalist school. . . . But Futurism remained within the Catholic ranks until much later. It did not permeate the ranks of Protestantism until the third decade of the nineteenth century" (Froom, vol. 4, p. 387).

We cannot underestimate the significance of the futurist approach to understanding Bible prophecy. It set a trend that ignored the positions originally held by the Protestant Reformers, and thousands upon thousands of evangelical Christians, most of whom haven't a clue as to the roots of their belief system, now known as "dispenstationalism" or belief in the "secret rapture," have embraced the concept.

Froom points out that of the 25 prominent writers between 1639 and the close of the seventeenth century, virtually all had a number of teachings in common: (a) they referred to the church-state Papacy as the antichrist; (b) they believed that they were living in the divided kingdom represented by the feet and toes of the image depicted in Daniel 2; and (c) they lived in expectation of the final, everlasting world-filling kingdom represented by the stone of Daniel 2:44, 45. They also believed that the 70-week period mentioned in Daniel 9:24 applied to the Jews and led up to the first advent of Christ (*ibid.*, vol. 3, p. 387).

Joseph Tanner aptly described the effect of the counter-reformation: "The Jesuit Ribera tried to set aside the application of these prophecies to the Papal Power by bringing out the *Futurist* system, which asserts that these prophecies refer properly not to the career of the Papacy, but to that of some future supernatural individual, who is yet to appear, and to continue in power for three and a half years. Thus, as Alford says, the Jesuit Ribera, about A.D. 1580, may be regarded as the Founder of the Futurist system of modern times" (Joseph Tanner, *Daniel and the Revelation,* pp. 16, 17; in Froom, vol. 2, p. 487).

In the nineteenth century Catholic futurism began to gain

influence in Britain. Protestant expositors, strange as it may seem, began to promote the old Jesuit position, thus breaking the force of the historic Reformation view regarding the church-state antichrist. Protestants now began to promote the teachings of men such as Bellarmine, regarded as "the most notable of the Jesuit controversialists and the greatest adversary of the Protestant churches" (Ladd, *The Blessed Hope,* p. 38).

Futurism could not be truly effective until it permeated Protestant thinking. The Jesuit victory was more complete than I'm sure Ribera or Bellarmine had ever dreamed possible. No longer does the Roman Catholic Church have to counter the Reformation approach to understanding prophecy.

John N. Darby, of the Plymouth Brethren, carried this theory to America on six visits to the New World, where Cyrus Ingerson Scofield eventually took it up. Born in 1843 and raised in the South, Scofield served in Robert E. Lee's Confederate army and received the Confederate Cross of Honor for his military service. After leaving the military, he became a lawyer, though it appears that he had something of an unsavory history.

The Topeka, Kansas, *Daily Capital,* in its August 27, 1881, issue, described him in highly unflattering terms. "Cyrus I. Scofield, formerly of Kansas, late lawyer, politician and shyster generally, has come to the surface again. . . . The last personal knowledge that Kansans have had of this peer among scalawags, was about four years ago, after a series of forgeries and confidence games, he left the state and a destitute family and took refuge in Canada.

"Shortly after he left Kansas, leaving his wife and two children dependent upon the bounty of his wife's mother, he wrote his wife that he could invest some $1,300.00 of her mother's money, all she had, in a manner that would return big interest. After some correspondence he forwarded them a mortgage, signed and executed by one Chas. Best, purporting to convey valuable property in St. Louis. Upon this, the money was sent to him. Afterwards, the mortgages were found to be base forgeries, no such person as Charles Best being in existence, and the property conveyed in the mortgage, fictitious" (in MacPherson, pp. 65, 74).

Scofield, it appears, spent some time in jail. The newspaper goes on to tell of how a group of missionaries from the St. Louis Flower Mission visited him in jail. One of them was a young woman whom he fell in love with and married. Even after his conversion, however, he seemed quite unconcerned about his first wife and children. According to the newspaper report, he obtained a divorce under false pretenses.

David MacPherson has researched Scofield's past, visiting his first wife's grave and reading old newspapers with accounts of his life. He found another stunning report in the December 28, 1899, issue of the Kansas City *Journal.* The article presents details of what it refers to as "Scofield's checkered life."

After his born-again experience, Scofield left his practice of law to become a pastor. He so impressed Dwight L. Moody that the evangelist asked him to pastor Moody's Congregational church in East Northfield, Massachusetts, which he did from 1895 to 1902. Seven years later Scofield published his *Reference Bible,* which through numerous notes presented dispensationalism and the doctrine of the secret rapture. Quickly the ideas infiltrated into fundamentalist Protestantism.

The *Scofield Reference Bible* was a monumental work, and it stands as one of the greatest promoters of futurism. Since its publication it has sold more than 2 million copies. An estimated several hundred "Bible Institutes" in the United States use the *Scofield Reference Bible* as their study guide. Their many hundreds of graduates have filled the pulpits of America and promoted the teaching of dispensationalism and the secret rapture—just as they have learned it from Scofield's famous Bible.

Many have associated Scofield's teachings with the sacred Word itself because his notes accompany the writings of Peter and Paul. William E. Cox has commented that "from a position of entire ignorance of the Scriptures, to a position of oracular religious certainty—especially respecting eschatological matters—for some people requires from three to six months with a Scofield Bible" (*An Examination of Dispensationalism,* p. 20).

At the end of his research, MacPherson concluded: "If believers had been able to examine his [Scofield's] deeds as much as his doctrines, the Scofield story might have had a different ending" (p. 81).

Many are unaware that the antichrist referred to by dispensationalists and those who believe in the secret rapture does not correspond well with the description found in Bible prophecy. The following passages could not possibly fit some future individual rising up in Jerusalem, because both John and Paul indicated that the antichrist was already beginning to work in their day—during the first century.

"This is that spirit of antichrist, whereof ye have heard that it should come; *and even now already is it in the world"* (1 John 4:3). "Let no man deceive you by any means: for that day shall not come, except there come a falling away first, and that man of sin be revealed, the son of perdition; who opposeth and exalteth himself above all that is called God, or that is worshipped; so that he as God sitteth in the temple of God, shewing himself that he is God. . . . *For the mystery of iniquity doth already work"* (2 Thessalonians 2:3-7).

Joseph Tanner was keenly aware of this problem, and his statement should give futurists something to think about as they abandon the historic prophetic insights and adopt any form of biblical interpretation that obscures the distinct biblical warnings given in prophecy: "It is a matter for deep regret that those who hold and advocate the futurist system at the present day, Protestants as they are for the most part, are really thus playing into the hands of Rome, and helping to screen the papacy from detection as the Antichrist. It has been well said that 'Futurism tends to obliterate the brand put by the Holy Spirit upon popery'" (*Daniel and the Revelation,* p. 16).

How conclusive is the historic Protestant position that identified the state-church Papacy, especially as it existed during the Middle Ages, as the antichrist? Is it idle speculation? Stay with us as we examine the characteristics of the power predicted in God's Word. When we compare the abundance of evidence given in Scripture with the testimony found in world history, there need be no question.

Chapter 5

AMPUTATED IMAGES AND ELASTIC MEASURING TAPES

Henry Feyerabend

As we have seen, the Bible nowhere speaks of a secret rapture—it just is not there. In order to understand the reasoning that leads to the teaching of the rapture, it is important to study the principles of Bible study used to arrive at this theory. Since we cannot find any obvious Bible description of an event held dear by so many Christians today, we must try to determine whether or not it is valid to postulate a secret rapture from the biblical data.

Dispensationalists claim that it is. William Harrison, admitting that the New Testament does not describe a secret rapture, has suggested that "it must be inferred from a careful analysis of those passages which are relevant" ("The Time of the Rapture as Indicated in Certain Scriptures," p. 318).

So let's look at some of the hermeneutic principles dispensationalism rests on.

The key to understanding futurist interpretation is what some have called "the gap theory" or "the great parenthesis." Harry Ironside has creatively described it as the stopping of the prophetic clock. He tells us that we live in a time not addressed by Bible prophecy. "The moment Messiah died on the cross, the prophetic clock stopped. There has not been a tick upon that clock for nineteen centuries. It will not begin again until the entire present age has come to an end and Israel will once more be taken up by God" (*The Great Parenthesis*, p. 23).

Secret rapture advocates have described understanding this parenthesis or gap as the "true key to a right understanding of prophecy" (*ibid.,* p. 13). Without this key the entire structure of dispensational eschatology would collapse.

Here is Ironside's concise description of the teaching of the parenthesis: "Between the sixty-ninth and seventieth weeks [of Daniel 9:24-27] we have a great parenthesis which has now lasted over nineteen hundred years. The seventieth week has been postponed by God Himself, who changes the times and the seasons because of the transgression of the people" (*ibid.,* p. 23).

Also according to this theory, chapters 6 to 19 of the book of Revelation describe the seventieth week of Daniel's prophecy. On this interpretation, we are now living in the gap, also called the "church age." This proposed parenthesis supposedly began on the day of Pentecost and allegedly will continue until the rapture, when the seventieth week will commence. The understanding of this principle "lays the foundation for a consistent interpretation of the Revelation" (H. C. Thiessen, *Will the Church Pass Through the Tribulation?* p. 26).

Dispensationalists regard the church age as a valley of prophecy that the prophets did not see. "They wrote, as Peter again tells us, of the suffering of Christ and the glories that should follow, but of the interval between the two they know nothing. The strange thing is that many Christians ignore it today, and by failing to recognize the importance of this great parenthesis, they are in continual perplexity as to the time when prophecy is to be fulfilled" (Ironside, p. 35).

The secret rapture concept regards the age in which we live as not in the line of vision of the Old Testament prophets. "The divine reckoning makes no place for this unforeseen and unpredicted age of grace, as it is manifested in the Church" (Lewis Sperry Chafer, *Systematic Theology,* vol. 4, p. 339).

Chafer also says—and notice his strange description—that "if this detached, disassociated, segregated character of this age is not granted, there can be tracing of God's time-periods as they are revealed" *(ibid.).*

"After nineteen centuries during which Christ had not returned physically to the earth how was it possible to vitalize the belief that He may now come at any moment? Dispensationalism has answered by saying that the nineteen centuries of the dispensation of grace or the church age, have been a parenthesis not covered by Bible prophecy, and that this interval may end at any moment, when the clock of prophecy will resume its ticking" (C. Norman Kraus, *Dispensationalism in America,* p. 8).

Where in the Bible do we find an indication of any "age of the church" gap? Yet Ironside points out that to recognize the break in the prophetic interpretation of Daniel is to see the possibility of finding this same break in many places throughout the Scriptures (Ironside, p. 27).

Someone has pointed out to me that the most obvious reference to the gap is in the fourth chapter of the Gospel of Luke. Jesus was reading from the sixty-first chapter of the book of Isaiah when He suddenly stopped reading in the middle of a sentence. According to this individual, by doing this He was introducing the Gospel era. He ceased reading as He uttered the words "To preach the acceptable year of the Lord" (Luke 4:19). According to this interpretation, He did not read further because the day of vengeance of our God was not due to begin at that time, and is indeed still future. This, to dispensationalists, clearly indicates a gap in prophecy. Even though a comma was not in the original manuscript, it is vitally important. Proponents of the secret rapture ask us to believe that by pausing in His reading, Jesus expected that every reader should understand that He was introducing a new and convoluted system of theology.

"In other words, *our Lord put the entire dispensation of the grace of God in which we live into a comma.* That comma represents a period of two thousand years at least. How much more we cannot say" (*ibid.,* pp. 28, 29).

Though Bible students throughout the centuries have not perceived this comma to be a period of 2,000 years, futurists find it so obvious that they regard it as strange that so many Bible students can't see it. Ironside assures us that so many references to this gap exist in the Scriptures that an attempt to refer to the ones only in the Psalms would require writing an entire book (*ibid.,* p. 43).

The gap is also supposed to be evident in Daniel 2, coming between the legs of iron (which dispensationalists do correctly interpret as representing Rome) and the feet of clay, which they regard as signifying 10 kings that will arise during the future seventieth week (*ibid.,* p. 37).

They also see the same interval in Daniel 7 as coming between the fourth beast, or the Roman Empire, and the 10 horns, or between verses 23 and 24. Proponents of the secret rapture also claim to detect it in Daniel 8, 11, and 12, and between the fifth and sixth chapters of Hosea. It interrupts Revelation 3 and 4 as well. Ironside says that "the thoughtful reader who searches the Scriptures in dependence upon the Spirit of God will have no difficulty in finding many more" (*ibid.,* p. 36).

When Daniel interpreted the dream of King Nebuchadnezzar, he was unaware that the image would be amputated between the legs and the feet. Nor did he know that the horns of the beast of Daniel 7 were not connected to the beast, but were separated by a 2,000-year gap. Dispensationalist scholars argue that Daniel didn't know that his 70-week prophecy was not really 70 weeks, but included a gap of at least 2,000 years.

Here is how Chafer explains it: "In the continuity of divine reckoning, the feet of iron and clay are attached and their representation follows the iron-leg period without interruption. Likewise, Daniel's seventieth week is in a sequence of 69 which have gone before and completes that belonging to the 69. Though 2,000 years fall in between, prophetic continuity sees only the Gentile realities represented by an unamputated image, and the Jewish history of 490 years unbroken by any unforeseen and unrelated age" (vol. 4, pp. 339, 340).

Chafer makes a most striking admission. Dispensationalism has inserted an element into the prophecies that the inspired prophets were totally unaware of. Yet the Bible declares: "Surely the Lord God will do nothing, but he revealeth his secret unto his servants the prophets" (Amos 3:7). According to the conclusions of many dispensationalist scholars, however, the entire

Christian dispensation, which they claim to be the key to unlock all prophecies, was totally unknown not only to the prophets, but also to all biblical scholars prior to the advent of futurism.

The writings of Philip Mauro expose the weakness in this type of reasoning. He maintains that making God's measuring line of the 70 weeks an elastic one completely frustrates the use of prophecy. The 70 weeks stretch out over thousands of years. Mauro says that "to postpone the seventieth week to the distant future makes shipwreck of the entire prophecy" (*The Seventy Weeks and the Great Tribulation*, p. 113). Then he goes on to maintain that "the seventieth week of prophecy occurred just where we would expect to find the seventieth number of any series, and that is next after the sixty-ninth" (*ibid.*, p. 113).

Suppose you should ask someone, "How far is it to Chicago?"

"Seventy miles," comes the answer.

You would naturally conclude that you could drive the distance in little more than an hour. But the individual then informs you that it will take you a number of days to drive that distance because a gap of 2,000 miles lurks between the sixty-ninth and seventieth mile. With such a gap in place, the distance would no longer be 70 miles, but 2,070.

Inserting a 2,000-year gap in the 70-week prophecy totally obliterates its meaning. Take away the seventieth week from the prophecy, and a plain and simple statement becomes devoid of meaning. Clearly such a method of interpretation makes nonsense of the time periods given, and it would follow that Daniel must have been miserably deceived in what he received from God and presented in his writings.

The deepest search fails to find basis for a parenthesis separating the sixty-ninth and seventieth weeks of Daniel 9. The fact is that the last week in this great important prophecy represents one of the most conclusive prophetic references in all of the Scriptures. In it we find supportive chronological evidence that Jesus was the Christ, the Messiah, who appeared in history at the right time according to God's great prophetic clock.

This prophecy, so marvelous in its simplicity and convincing in its testimony, met its fulfillment in that eventful week of years beginning with Jesus' ministry starting at His baptism in

A.D. 27 (the fifteenth year of Tiberius Caesar); centering in His crucifixion (A.D. 30 or 31); and ending with the stoning of Stephen in A.D. 34, when the good news of salvation began to spread to the Gentiles.

In the words of Varner J. Johns: "How fantastic, how fanciful is the idea of those who would detach this last week from the seventy and arbitrarily assign it to a period two thousand years in the future" (*The Secret Rapture and the Antichrist,* p. 80).

What is behind this scheme? Is it part of a great cover-up? It is a component of a sinister conspiracy that has beguiled the fundamentalist and evangelical Christian world and obscured the prophecies that God so clearly presented for our warning and admonition in the final days of the history of the world.

By placing the Christian Era in a parenthesis, or gap, Christian preachers claim that our day was invisible to the prophets and that we are behind a hill over which God's spokespeople could not see. In practice, this prevents most any person, power, kingdom, or religious movement from being identified by biblical prophecy.

And the best that we can tell from the historical record, it was done deliberately! The finger of prophecy pointed directly at a religious phenomena or mentality, not an individual person. The Reformers in their Bible study clearly understood the impact of this message, but Satan saw that they were getting much too close to identifying this power. Something had to be done— and something was done. It's a story of intrigue and treachery!

Chapter 6

RULES AND EXCEPTIONS TO RULES

Henry Feyerabend

I f the plain sense makes good sense, seek no other sense, or you will learn nonsense" has been presented as a motto of dispensational theology. One of the features of dispensationalism is what its advocates call "plain hermeneutics," referred to by some theologians as "wooden literalism." Dispensationalists claim to accept prophecies literally.

"Dispensationalism is a result of consistent application of the basic hermeneutical principle of literal, normal, or plain interpretation. No other system of theology can claim this" (Charles Caldwell Ryrie, *Dispensationalism Today,* p. 96).

Admittedly, there is much to be said in favor of accepting the Bible just as it reads. Many theological problems have resulted from overspiritualizing passages that could have and should have been taken in their normal sense. But when John Walvoord says that "the major differences between amillennialism and premillennialism★ lie in the use of the literal method of interpretation" (*The Rapture Question,* p. 56), he is not referring to an ordinary acceptance of Bible truths at their face value, but rather to a rigid, hyperliteral interpretation of all prophecy, especially the Old Testament kingdom prophecies.

Secret rapturists appeal to reason to argue in favor of their hermeneutic principle. They state that God, as the author of language, gave us the use of language for the purpose of communication. Furthermore, He gave us sufficient language to convey "all that was in His heart to tell man" (Ryrie, pp. 87, 88). Consequently, we would expect God to use language in its literal, normal, and plain sense. So far, so good. It's hard to argue with that.

"If language is the creation of God for the purpose of conveying His message, then a theist must view that language as sufficient in scope and normative in use in accomplishing that purpose" *(ibid.)*.

Charles L. Feinberg explains it this way: "Spiritualizers find it hard to explain—and no one has successfully attempted it—why the Scriptures do not mean what they say and why they do not say what they mean. Is it not strange that God who called light into existence with two words should not be able to say what He means?" (*Premillennialism or Amillennialism?* 2nd ed., p. 41).

The inference is that unless we accept everything in the Bible as literal, we become guilty of doubting God's ability to express Himself. But such wooden literalism in reading the Bible just does not work, because it ends up making nonsense of what Scripture says. When Scripture states that God is a rock—one that gives birth at that (Deuteronomy 32:18)—are we to understand this literally, that God is lifeless and hard, maybe made of limestone or granite, yet gives birth to—what? to other rocks?

And as we shall see, dispensationalists are not—nor could they be—consistent in applying their principle. Few would question God's divine ability to express Himself. The problem is one of human capacity to understand what He says. Even Christ said that He had much to tell the disciples, but they could not grasp it at the time.

"Why speakest thou unto them in parables?" (Matthew 13:10) the disciples asked Jesus. They couldn't understand why He did not say what He meant to say in plain words. Like Jesus, many of the prophets spoke in symbolic language. Some were living as exiles or prisoners, and their prophecies would never have reached us had they not presented them in symbolic language. Another reason for God to couch certain prophecies in symbolic language is for the purpose of illustration.

Clarence Bass has pointed out that pressing the principle of literalness in a rigid and unyielding manner can actually pervert the meaning of the text (*Backgrounds to Dispensationalism,* pp. 20, 21). Too much literalness can be just as hazardous as too much symbolism. William E. Cox points this out: "It is theological pandemonium to attempt to take an either-or approach to all Scriptures. One must recognize both literal and spiritual descendants" (*An Examination of Dispensationalism,* p. 26).

It is impossible to study the Scriptures and be as woodenly literal as dispensationalists recommend. No consistent and rigid literalists really exist, not even among dispensationalists. Even their theologians fall into spiritualizing. For example, their founder, John Darby, interpreted the resurrection of Daniel 12 as spiritual, a figurative resurrection of the people buried as a nation among the Gentiles *(ibid.).*

The book of Revelation describes Christ's arriving on a white horse, crowned with many diadems, garbed in a robe dipped in blood, accompanied by the armies of heaven on white horses, and coming to smite the nations with a sword that sticks out of His mouth. No dispensationalist would ever deny that it consists of symbolic language.

In one of his books Oswald Smith announces: "Nor are we going to dishonor God by spiritualizing [the Scripture writers'] utterances. We take them just as they read" (in Cox, p. 27). Then, in the same book, he goes on to identify the "branch" as symbolizing Jesus Christ, and he says that "a mountain in prophecy is a kingdom" (in Cox, p. 27). Does that sound like he takes every word of Scripture literally?

W. W. Barndollar says of Scripture that "it must be interpreted according to the normal, historical, socially accustomed use of the language" (*The Validity of Dispensationalism,* p. 26). A little later in his book we find this interpretation: "Consider Psalm 1:12. Notice what it says: 'Kiss the Son.' Here is God's instruction to the nations that are in revolt against Him today. 'Kiss the Son.' What does He mean? Read the passage. He is saying, 'Get saved and accept Christ as Saviour'" (*ibid.,* p. 61). Hardly is he using the "normal, historical, socially accustomed" use of the word "kiss."

Speaking of the description of Christ in the first chapter of Revelation, E. Schuyler English, a dispensationalist writer, comments: "To suppose that the Lord Jesus actually looked like the being described so strikingly in this passage is to be grossly misled. Several medieval artists tried to put on canvas a portrait of Christ from the minute details of this Scripture passage. But their handiwork has left us nothing except monstrous caricatures of Him who is the Head of creation" (in Charles Lee Feinberg, ed., *Prophecy and the Seventies*, p. 77).

The same writer, speaking of the 24 elders mentioned in the last book of the Bible, writes: "These twenty-four elders in heaven represent the whole church" (in Feinburg, *Prophecy and the Seventies*, p. 61). He goes on to say that 12 of the elders stand for the saved Jews, and the other 12 the Gentiles.

Charles Ryrie urges rigid literal interpretation by declaring that "a second reason why dispensationalists believe in the literal principle is a Biblical one. It is simply this: the prophecies in the Old Testament concerning the first coming of Christ—His birth, His rearing, His ministry, His death, His resurrection— were all fulfilled literally. There is no non-literal fulfillment of these prophecies in the New Testament. This argues strongly for the literal method" (*Dispensationalism Today*, p. 146).

George L. Murray responds to this statement when he observes that "we have to say in all charity that this statement lacks due consideration" (*Millennial Studies*, p. 27). Murray goes on to point out just a few examples of symbolic language in prophecy that have already been fulfilled in regard to the first coming of Christ. A prime example would be Genesis 3:15, in which we have the first promise of a Savior. Most Christians agree that it has been fulfilled in Christ, yet none would say that a snake literally bruised His heel or that He literally crushed a serpent's head.

Scholars generally accept Psalm 22 as a prophetic description of our Lord's passion. "Many bulls have compassed me: strong bulls of Bashan have beset me round" (verse 12). "For dogs have compassed me" (verse 16). "Save me from the lion's mouth: for thou hast heard me from the horns of unicorns" (verse 21). Would any dispensationalist scholar claim this prophecy to be literal?

It doesn't take too much study to see that all Old Testament prophecies concerning the first coming of Christ were not literal.

According to dispensationalists, one of the most appealing features of literal interpretation is its consistency. But because it is impossible to interpret every passage of Scripture literally, they have had to generate exceptions to the rule. Scofield stated that "it is then permitted—while holding firmly the historical verity—reverently to spiritualize the historic Scriptures. [In the prophetic scriptures] we reach the ground of absolute literalness. Figures are often found in prophecies, but the figure invariably has a literal fulfillment. Not one instance exists of a 'spiritual' or 'figurative' fulfillment of prophecy" (The *Scofield Correspondence Course;* in Fuller, *Hermeneutics,* p. 150).

We have already offered some examples of prophecies that no rational person, including dispensationalists, would attempt to claim were literally fulfilled. John Darby offered yet another exception to the rule of plain hermeneutics, even when dealing with prophetic Scriptures: "When the Jewish church or nation (exclusive of the Gentile parenthesis in their history) is concerned, i.e. when the address is directly to the Jews, there we may look for a plain and direct testimony, because earthly things were the Jew's proper portion. And, on the contrary, where the address is to the Gentiles, i.e. when the Gentiles are concerned in it, there we may look for a symbol, because earthly things were not their portion" (*On Days Signifying Years in Prophetic Language [Collected Writings],* pp. 11, 53, 54, in Fuller, p. 150).

Confusing, isn't it? Gone are the consistency and objectivity of the rule. Only when it refers to prophecy, and then only when addressed to the Jews, does God say what He means and mean what He says. To decide which teaching is a "kingdom teaching" and which is a "church teaching" must be left to the discretion of the dispensationalist as he or she interprets all Scripture.

C. Norman Kraus observes that "literal Old Testament history is often treated figuratively, while prophecy is interpreted literally. . . . Both are used outside of their true historical content" (*Dispensationalism in America,* p. 9).

It is this situation that has left dispensationalists vulnerable to sharp comments. One by Clarence G. Bass is typical: "Dispensationalists will not interpret the obviously literal as literal, and the obviously symbolic as symbolic. Everything must be literal. R.C.H. Lenski, noted for his hermeneutic scholarship, characterizes this type of interpretation as follows: 'What is so depressing about the bulk of this exegesis is its unexegetical character. Even words are not allowed to mean what they naturally and always mean. The presentation of the sound exegetes are ignored as though they did not exist. A sort of willful resistance against what is even obvious pervades the majority'" (*Backgrounds,* pp. 23, 24).

The rigidity of dispensationalists in refusing to recognize the spiritual Israel spoken of in the New Testament is an example of the hyperliteralism that obscures the true meaning of Bible passages.

Dispensationalists claim that literalism is a "logical rationale," and they ask: "What check would there be on the variety of interpretations which man's imagination could produce if we do not adhere to this method of interpretation?" (Ryrie, p. 88).

As we study their literature, we find that their wooden literalism is not an effective control. A sample reading of their literature, such as the *Left Behind* series of books, shows that nothing keeps their imagination from running rampant.

The truth is that some prophetic passages obviously contain figurative language. Others the New Testament itself gives a figurative interpretation. Still others, if taken literally, would contradict truths and principles or even factual statements contained in nonsymbolic books of the New Testament. Unless one of the above conditions exists, we would agree to use the normal literal sense of the passage. Beyond this, even the dispensationalists cannot go.

The Protestant Reformers recognized the importance of symbolism in prophecy. In 1617 Richard Bernard, a Puritan, aptly stated the need to look beyond the letter and "the naked relation of things as they are set down." He said that without recognizing this, we would have a book full of "absurdities and impossibilities, falsities and flat contradictions. For who can believe a lamb to have seven eyes, a mountain burning to be cast into the sea, locusts to be of so monstrous a shape as is set down in chapter IX, and horses with lions' heads, fire, smoke and brimstone coming out of their mouths, and a hundred such things?" (*A Key of Knowledge for the Opening of the Secret Mysteries of St. John's Mystical Revelation,* pp. 130, 131).

The principle of hyperliteralism can easily disguise the true meaning of prophecy. The incidentals become so important that they cloud the real issues. Speaking of the mark in the forehead or right hand as referred to in Revelation 13, Hal Lindsey declares: "Everyone will be given a tattoo or mark on either his forehead or forehand, only if he swears allegiance to the dictator as being God" (*The Late Great Planet Earth,* pp. 112, 113).

But the prophecy has in mind far greater issues than a literal stamp that someone forces people to have on their skin. God is more concerned with the heart than He is with a little bit of ink. The narrow, literal interpretation hides the true meaning of the prophecy. Some point to computers and Social Security numbers, when God directs us to the great question of loyalty. The issue is literally more than skin-deep.

---

* Dispensationalists often use the term *premillennialism* to refer to dispensationalism, though many premillennialists are not pretribulationalists.

Chapter 7

EXTRA BAGGAGE

Henry Feyerabend

A man at Los Angeles International Airport worried that he would miss his plane. He had no wristwatch and could not locate a clock. Then he saw a stranger approaching with two heavy suitcases. "Why do people travel with such heavy baggage?" he murmured to himself. He prided himself on traveling light. Walking up to the stranger, he said, "Excuse me; could you give me the time, please?"

The stranger smiled and said, "Sure." Setting down the two large suitcases, he looked at the watch on his wrist. "It is exactly 5:09. The temperature outside is 73 degrees, and it is supposed to rain tonight. In London the sky is clear and the temperature is 38 degrees Celsius. The barometer reading there is 29.14 and falling. And, let me see, in Singapore the sun is shining brightly. Oh, by the way, the moon should be full tonight here in Los Angeles, and . . . "

"Your watch tells you all that?" the man interrupted.

"Oh, yes. And much more. You see, I invented this watch, and I can assure you there is no other timepiece like it in the world."

"I want to buy that watch! I'll pay you $2,000 for it right now."

"No, it's not for sale," said the stranger as he reached down to pick up his suitcases.

"Wait! Four thousand dollars. I'll pay you $4,000 cash," the man offered, reaching for his wallet.

"No, I can't sell it. You see, I plan to give it to my son for his twenty-first birthday. I invented it for him to enjoy."

"OK, listen. I'll give you $10,000. I've got the money right here."

The stranger paused. "Ten thousand dollars? Well, OK. It's yours for $10,000 even."

The purchaser was absolutely elated. Paying the stranger, he took the watch, snapped it on his wrist with glee, said, "Thanks," and turned to leave.

"Wait," said the stranger. With a big smile he handed the two heavy suitcases to the man and added, "Don't forget the batteries."

Hermeneutical rules should simplify the study and understanding of Scripture. When they make the meaning of the Bible become obscure and complicated, they have lost their usefulness. Many who believe in the secret rapture of the church do not realize what teachings they inherit along with this belief. They do not know how bogged down they will become if they follow their beliefs to their logical conclusion.

One cannot truly follow the conventional forms of Christianity and be a true dispensationalist. Many dispensationalists, for example, have taught that not only the Old Testament, but also the major part of the New Testament, was not addressed to Christians at all, but exclusively to the Jewish nation. As a result they reject many of the most beautiful teachings of Christ.

Dispensationalism rests on two hermeneutical principles. One is wooden literalism, discussed in the previous chapter. The second is the assumption that throughout the ages God has pursued two distinct purposes: one related to the earth with earthly people and earthly objectives (Judaism); the other related to heaven with heavenly people and heavenly objectives (Christianity).

Thus some have classified the Sermon on the Mount in the category of kingdom teachings, implying that it was not meant for Christians. A Christian who repeats the Lord's Prayer or who lives by the golden rule or who claims the blessings of the Beatitudes would thus be out of harmony with dispensational theology.

"Since the believer is so clearly delivered from the law, he cannot be governed by the Sermon on the Mount, for it is legal in character. The admitted legality of this discourse, conceded even by those who apply these words to the believer today, makes it impossible to hold that position" (J. Dwight Pentecost, "The Purpose of the Sermon on the Mount," *Bibliotheca Sacra* CXV [1958]: 132).

Speaking of the Lord's Prayer, Lewis Sperry Chafer once commented: "'And forgive us our debts as we forgive our debtors.' . . . This, again, is purely legal. Forgiveness on the part of the Christian is enjoined; but it is enjoined in agreement with the exalted principle of grace. . . . The legal character of this great kingdom-prayer should not be overlooked because of sentimental reasons growing out of early training" (*Systematic Theology,* vol. 4. p. 221).

He also wrote about the Beatitudes: "These blessings are won through merit. This is in sharp contrast to the blessings in the exalted position of the Christian to which he instantly attains through Christ at the moment he believes" (*ibid.,* p. 216).

Fortunately, not all dispensationalists go along with the founding principles of dispensationalism. Charles R. Swindoll, president of Dallas Theological Seminary, a citadel of dispensationalism, wrote a book called *Simple Faith.* In it he strongly applied the Sermon on the Mount to Christians, calling this beautiful Bible teaching "The Everest of Ethics," "The Cornerstone of True Christianity," and "The Capstone of Jesus' Sermon" (p. 215).

Evidently Chuck Swindoll and other recent dispensationalists are not willing to carry the extra baggage of having to exclude large portions of the teachings of Jesus from Christianity. Yet some have considered this separation of kingdom teaching from Christian teachings as the real test of dispensationalism. Charles Caldwell Ryrie called it the sine qua non of dispensationalism. He regarded it as the most conclusive test of whether or not a person is a dispensationalist. "A man who fails to distinguish Israel and the church will inevitably not hold to dispensational distinction; and one who does will" (*Dispensationalism Today,* p. 48).

Swindoll refers to the golden rule as "the best part of the

whole principle." "Living by the Golden Rule prevents the need for laying down an endless list of little rules and regulation to govern conduct," he comments. "Just put yourself in the other person's place and think, 'What is it I would need if I were him or her?' And then? Do it. When you do, you will fulfill the essence of 'the law and the Prophets'" (*Simple Faith,* p. 216).

In total contrast Chafer, one of the former theologians of the school Swindoll now directs, said of the golden rule: "The legal principle, restated in this passage, is not said to be any part of the teachings of grace: it is rather 'the law and the prophets'" (*Systematic Theology,* vol. 4, p. 224).

According to some proponents of dispensationalism, we must not all appear before the judgment seat of Christ, as Paul suggests. Once a person has accepted Christ they will not have to give an account of their words or deeds, but have passed beyond all judgment.

"'Judge not, that ye be not judged. For with what judgment ye judge, ye shall be judged: and with what measure ye mete, it shall be measured to you again.' One under grace has passed beyond all judgment, by virtue of his acceptance in Christ who died for him" (*ibid.,* p. 223). On the other hand, some dispensationalists call for multiple judgments.

Chafer rejected even such teachings as faithfulness and endurance when he wrote: "Under the conditions laid down in the kingdom teachings, life is entered by a personal faithfulness. . . . 'But he that shall endure unto the end, the same shall be saved' (Matt. 24:13); but nothing could be more contradictory to the teachings of grace than the principle set forth in this passage" (*ibid.,* pp. 224, 225).

He also admonished the Christian to avoid any part of the Sermon on the Mount or any part of the Law of Moses. To accept a part of it, he argued, is to place oneself under obligation to accept it all, including the sacrifices of the ceremonial law. "The teachings of Moses and the teachings of the kingdom are purely legal, while the instructions to the believer of this dispensation are in conformity with pure grace. . . . The law cannot be broken or divided. It stands as a unit. To undertake any part of it is to be committed to it all. Nothing could be more unreasonable or unscriptural than to borrow some portions from the law system, either that of Moses or of the kingdom, and, at the same time, reject other portions" (*ibid.*, p. 225).

It seems difficult to know how any Christian, or any decent citizen of the land for that matter, could possibly avoid undertaking any part of the moral law or the teachings of Jesus in the Sermon on the Mount. Yet Chafer considered it unreasonable and illogical to live by the golden rule unless one adhered to the sacrifices of the Old Testament. "The kingdom law is a complete and indivisible system in itself. It is therefore unscriptural, illogical, and unreasonable to appropriate convenient and pleasing portions of this law, and to neglect the remainder" (*ibid.*, p. 245).

John Darby had earlier stated that "nothing indeed was addressed to the church by the Lord in person, because the church did not yet exist to be addressed" (W. Kelly, ed., *The Collected Writings of J. N. Darby*, vol. 4, p. 31). And J. C. O'Hair, another dispensationalist teacher, claimed that "there is not a thimble-full of grace in the synoptic Gospels" (J. C. O'Hair, *The Great Blunder of the Church*, in W. E. Cox, *Examination of Dispensationalism*, p. 41).

Chafer even went so far as to argue that "there is a dangerous and entirely baseless sentiment abroad which assumes that every teaching of Christ must be binding during this age simply because Christ said it" (*Systematic Theology*, vol. 4, p. 224). It's almost impossible to imagine that a Christian theologian would say such a thing!

Instead of directing people to the Bible and the teachings of Jesus, radical dispensationalism took most of the words of Jesus away from Christianity. Yet the Sermon on the Mount is not some peripheral matter. It constitutes the very heart of our Lord's teachings.

To illustrate just where this type of reasoning can lead, Korean Christians used an extreme dispensational hermeneutic as an excuse for bowing at shrines dedicated to the sun goddess, the mythical ancestor of the Japanese emperor, even though they admitted that it broke both the first and second commandments (Floyd E. Hamilton, *The Basis of Millennial Faith*, pp. 27-29, in *Seventh-day Adventist Bible Students' Source Book*, p. 348).

Fortunately for society, few dispensationalists carry the

teachings of the late Dr. Chafer to their logical conclusion. Many, if not most, dispensationalists believe that Christians should be good, clean-living citizens just as Christ taught in the Sermon on the Mount and just as the moral law as spelled out in the Ten Commandments indicates. It is refreshing that Barndollar insists: "Lying, cheating, stealing and immorality and any kind of sin that we meet, should have no part in our lives" (*Validity*, p. 64).

George Eldon Ladd's observation on the dispensationalist rejection of many parts of the Bible, claiming that they are not addressed to Christians, expresses the dangers of this position: "It is immediately obvious that a system which takes this greatest portion of Jesus' teaching away from the Christian in its direct application must receive a penetrating scrutiny. This is the reason the dispensational interpretation of the kingdom concerns us so vitally. When Christians will not use the Lord's Prayer because it is given for the kingdom age and not for the present age, we must test carefully the validity of the position" (*Crucial Questions,* p. 106).

Those dispensationalists who divide the Bible into compartments lose many blessings that God intended for Christians. They assign every verse in the Bible either to (a) the Jews, (b) the Gentiles, or (c) the church. We might well wonder why they don't publish a Bible in three sections, giving Christians only the portion that pertains to them. Such a Bible would, of course, be very small, containing only the writings of Paul and the first three chapters of Revelation.

Be aware, though, that the moment anyone decides to reject the major part of the Bible, it is impossible for a person to receive the full message of the Scriptures.

Yet more serious than all of this is the implication that large segments of Jesus' own teachings contradict the gospel of grace that He Himself came to initiate. The Bible clearly indicates that there is only one salvation. Without Christ's sacrifice, no person could or can be saved under any conditions.

Yet dispensationalism has taught that the Bible contains two distinct methods of salvation. "With the call of Abraham and the giving of the Law and all that has followed, there are two widely different, standardized, divine provisions, whereby man, who is utterly fallen, might come into the favor of God," Chafer claimed ("Dispensationalism," *Bibliotheca Sacra* XCIII [1936]: 410).

"Under grace, the fruit of the Spirit *is,* which indicates the present possession of the blessing through pure grace; while under the kingdom, the blessing *shall be* to such as merit it by their own works" (Chafer, *Systematic Theology,* vol. 4, p. 219).

But since the Bible clearly states that all have sinned and none are worthy of salvation, if in the kingdom only those who "merit it by their own works" will be saved, then everyone will be lost! The entire testimony of Scripture is that God has provided only *one* means of salvation, and that came through Calvary. If there were any other means, Christ's death would have been an unnecessary and useless sacrifice.

But Chafer carried his point even further. "In this age, God is dealing with men on the ground of His grace as it is in Christ. His dealings with men in the coming age are based on a very different relationship. At that time, the King will rule with a rod of iron. There is no word of the cross, or of grace, in the kingdom teachings" *(ibid.,* p. 222).

His teaching echoes that of C. I. Scofield. Here is a statement found in the notes of the 1917 edition of his Bible: "As a dispensation, grace begins with the death and resurrection of Christ (Rom. 3:24-26; 4:24, 25). The point of testing is no longer legal obedience as the condition of salvation, but acceptance or rejection of Christ" (*Scofield Reference Bible,* p. 1115).

Newer editions no longer contain the statement because of its obvious implications. The new edition of the *Scofield Reference Bible* declares instead: "Prior to the cross man's salvation was through faith (Gen. 15:6; Rom. 4:3), being grounded on Christ's atoning sacrifice, viewed anticipatively by God" (p. 1124).

While we can concur with it, on the same page of Scofield's notes we find a contradiction to the above statement and a reiteration of the former: "As a principle, therefore, grace is set in contrast with law (Rom. 11:6), under which God demands righteousness from men, as under grace, He gives righteousness to men" *(ibid.).*

To suggest the law as a "merit system" by which humans

could find favor with God in contrast to grace or unmerited favor is to contradict the plainest teachings of Scripture. "By the deeds of the law there shall no flesh be justified" (Romans 3:20).

"The law stands as the representation of the merit system—that divine arrangement which, according to New Testament, is held as the antipodes of God's plan of salvation by grace," Chafer continued. "Beyond the one truth that both systems are ordained of God for application in such ages as He may elect, they set up contrasts at every point" (*Systematic Theology,* vol. 3, p. 343).

The teaching of "two systems" of salvation contradicts the Word of God. No matter how hard its proponents try, dispensationalism cannot escape the taint of a double standard, because the principle of separation of the church from the kingdom carries with it elements of dual methods of salvation. Those who accept the prophetic interpretations of the *Scofield Reference Bible* inherit a baggage of theological implications that most Christians, even today's dispensationalists, cannot accept.

Compartmentalizing the Scriptures destroys the blessings of countless passages. It becomes extremely difficult to study the Bible, as the reader must assign every verse to one of the three categories—a difficult task at best. As we have already pointed out, in order to make the Bible readable it would be necessary to assign each verse to (a) the Jews, (b) the Gentiles, or (c) the church. Someone has suggested, probably tongue-in-cheek, that dispensationalists would perform a genuine service if they published the Bible in three different sections—or maybe three separate Bibles would work better.

The very moment dispensationalists distinguish two separate purposes for separate peoples in the Bible, they make it less possible to listen to all that the Bible has to say. Church truth must be interpreted as having no relation to the truth for the Jews, and vice versa. Although a theme in one compartment of the Bible might appear to be helpful to understanding another passage in what the dispensationalist considers to be a different compartment, they must automatically reject the possibility.

Chapter 8

O JERUSALEM

Henry Feyerabend

I t is said that the city of Jerusalem has a cage in which a wolf and a lamb live together, fulfilling the prophecy of Isaiah 65:25.

The story is told of a visit to Jerusalem during the time Richard Nixon was president of the United States. According to the story, Nixon said to secretary of state Henry Kissinger, "I want you to talk to the zookeeper and find out how he has been able to make peace between a wolf and a lamb. Maybe we can learn a lesson that will help us make peace between Israel and her Arab neighbors."

Kissinger approached the zookeeper with his question. "It is easy," the person told him. "We replace the lamb every day."

An anxious, tension-filled world watches Israel like a bomb in a crowded room. This country, sometimes referred to as the crossroads of the world, has a story written in blood. Tragedy on a gigantic scale has loomed over it for long centuries. It has felt the tramping hosts of many an army, including the legions of Nebuchadnezzar, Darius, Alexander the Great, the Ottoman Turks, and the British. Many armies have invaded it, including those of Christianity and Islam.

Located at the crossroads of Europe, Asia, and Africa, this land has always been filled with tension. Someone has said, "Pharaoh tried to drown Israel, but they would not drown.

Nebuchadnezzar tried to burn them, but they would not burn. Haman tried to hang them, but they would not hang."

An old slab of granite has a claim made by the Egyptian king Merneptah some 3,000 years ago: "Israel will have no posterity." Where is Merneptah today?

A German encyclopedia from the time of Hitler says: "In less than 100 years the Jewish problem will be solved." Where is Hitler today? He doesn't even have a tomb, whereas Israel still dominates the headlines of the world.

Dean Inge, of St. Paul's Cathedral in London, once said, "The Jews have always lived to stand at the graveside of their enemies." The Amorites, the Hittites, the Philistines, the Assyrians, and the Babylonians attacked them. Where are these nations today? How many Hittites do you know? How many Amorites or Babylonians do you hear about in the evening news?

One day King Frederick of Prussia spoke to one of his clergymen. "Tell me," he inquired. "What is the greatest evidence that the Bible is inspired?"

Without hesitation the clergyman replied, "The Jews, Your Majesty; the Jews."

On May 14, 1948, David Ben-Gurion read the Declaration of Independence announcing the establishment of a Jewish nation to be known as the State of Israel. Hal Lindsey referred to this as "one event which many Bible students in the past overlooked" (*The Late Great Planet Earth,* p. 43). Lindsey referred to it as a "paramount prophetic sign," assuring his readers that the next two prophetic signs to prepare the world for the rapture and the seven-year tribulation would be the Jews' repossession of Old Jerusalem and the rebuilding of the temple on Mount Moriah (*ibid.,* pp. 50, 51, 55, 56).

"Premillenarians expect the headlines to announce one day that Christ has come to rule and set up His kingdom on earth, that the Jewish people are dwelling safely in the promised land, and that the throne of David, occupied by the Son of David, has been established in Jerusalem. That will be the complete fulfillment of God's promise" (Charles C. Ryrie, *The Bible and Tomorrow's Headlines,* p. 81).

An earthly, Jewish kingdom is the millennial picture that

dispensationalists see in the Scriptures. They believe that the millennium will be the literal fulfillment of the Old Testament prophecies concerning the kingdom of the Jewish people.

According to Scofield, the "kingdom of God" and the "kingdom of heaven" are different things. The kingdom of heaven, he believed, is earthly and refers to the restoration of the Jews in Palestine. It is a limited term that refers to the millennium mentioned in the book of Revelation. The kingdom of God, he taught, is a "great inclusive expression" (in Theodore H. Epp, ed., *Brief Outlines of Things to Come*, p. 84) that includes the entire sphere in which God rules. Of the kingdom of heaven, Scofield said: "It is always limited to the earth; that is its sphere, even though glorified saints of this age and the past ages are concerned with it" (in Epp).

Scofield went on to illustrate that the kingdom of heaven is *in* the kingdom of God just as Texas is *in* the United States. Texas may have many features in common with the United States, such as the same language, the same president, and the same laws, but it must never become synonymous with the United States. So we may find many characteristics common between the kingdom of God and the kingdom of heaven, but they are always separate.

However, a fair examination of the Bible references to the kingdom fails to support Scofield's hypothesis, the basis for his millennial teachings.

Matthew in his account of the blessing of the children quotes Jesus Christ as declaring: "Suffer little children, and forbid them not, to come unto me: for of such is the *kingdom of heaven*" (Matthew 19:13). Mark's account of the same incident has Christ stating: "Suffer the little children to come unto me, and forbid them not: for of such is the *kingdom of God*" (Mark 10:14). Such parallelism suggests that they are one and the same thing. More than that, Christ uses the two terms interchangeably—as synonyms.

"Then said Jesus unto his disciples, Verily I say unto you, That a rich man shall hardly enter into the *kingdom of heaven*. And again I say unto you, it is easier for a camel to go through the eye of a needle, than for a rich man to enter into the *kingdom of God*" (Matthew 19:23, 24).

In the Gospels Jesus does not differentiate between two kinds of kingdoms, nor do the Scriptures anywhere else. Biblical scholars recognize from other first-century documents that the Jews frequently substituted the word "heaven" for the word "God." They thought they would thus avoid taking God's name in vain.

Yet Chafer argued: "All this [confusing of the kingdom of heaven with the kingdom of God] is but the dregs of Whitby's theory, which persuasion has so woefully ignored the precise teachings of the Bible" (*Systematic Theology,* vol. 5, p. 333).

Contemporary scholarship would beg to disagree with him, however. In discussing the terms *kingdom of God* and *kingdom of heaven, Harper's Bible Dictionary* asserts: "'Heaven' in these instances is a circumlocution—a way of referring to God without using his name. . . . Thus, 'Kingdom of Heaven' and 'Kingdom of God' are identical in meaning" (p. 528).

The entry in the *Zondervan Pictorial Encyclopedia of the Bible* agrees: "The two phrases are undoubtedly synonymous" (vol. 3, p. 803). Similarly, *The Illustrated Bible Dictionary* published by InterVarsity Press and Tyndale House states: "Mark and Luke speak of the 'kingdom of God', which has the same meaning as the 'kingdom of heaven', but was more intelligible to non-Jews" (vol. 2, p. 853).

The idea of separating the kingdom of heaven from the kingdom of God forms the basis for the postponement theory. It claims that when Christ came to the earth at His first advent, He intended to establish His literal earthly kingdom on the throne of David. He offered this kingdom to the Jews, but they rejected it, and the cross was the result.

"Jesus Christ was born 'King of the Jews,' but His nation rejected Him at that time" (W. W. Barndollar, *Validity,* p. 70). "The kingdom of heaven is the reign of heaven's King on earth. This Jesus offered to the nation of Israel when He came the first time, but they rejected it and He went to the cross" (M. R. DeHaan, *Second Coming,* p. 98).

"This offer was a bona fide offer, and had they received Him as their King, the nation's hopes would have been realized" (Chafer, *The Kingdom in History and Prophecy,* p. 56, in

W. E. Cox, *Examination,* p. 34). In other words, if the Jews had accepted Christ as their King, there would have been no Calvary experience, and the many Messianic prophecies would never have been fulfilled. According to this theory, the cross did not form part of God's original plan of salvation, but was something of an afterthought. Had the Jews accepted Christ's offer of an earthly kingdom, salvation would not have depended on the blood of Jesus.

Here is how one dispensational theologian has stated the matter: "It can be said at once that His dying was not God's own plan. It was conceived somewhere else and yielded to by God. God has a plan of atonement by which men who were willing could be saved from sin and its effect. That plan is given in the Old Hebrew Code. To the tabernacle or temple, under prescribed regulations, a man could bring some animal which he owned. The man brought that which was his own. It represented him. There is no cross in God's plan of atonement" (S. D. Gordon, *Quiet Talks About Jesus,* p. 131, in Cox, p. 31).

Once again we come across the legalism of dispensationalism, teaching that salvation could exist under the law. But it makes Christ's sacrifice a useless waste, because an animal could have done just as well.

A study of God's Word does not seem to indicate that Christ had any high kingly plans when He came to our world. From His lowly birth in a manger to His triumphant entrance into Jerusalem riding on an ass, and to His crucifixion on Calvary, He conveyed the message, "My kingdom is not of this world" (John 18:36). Nor was the cross an afterthought, for the Messianic prophecies of the Old Testament clearly foretold it.

It is hardly likely that the Jews would have spurned an earthly kingdom. What they rejected was a Messiah who disappointed them by not carrying out their expectations. Had they studied the prophecies more carefully, they might have known that the arrival of the Messiah would be twofold. They would have read about His sufferings, His coming in meekness and humility as "a man of sorrows, and acquainted with grief" (Isaiah 53:3). He was "wounded for our transgressions, he was bruised for our iniquities: the chastisement of our peace was upon him;

and with his stripes we are healed" (verse 5).

Dispensationalism orients itself more toward the Abrahamic covenant than the cross. Its focus centers not on the body of Christ—the church—but on the Jewish kingdom. Instead of interpreting the Old Testament prophecies in the light of the New Testament, it does just the opposite—interprets the New Testament in the light of the Old.

Clarence Bass clearly points out this fact when he makes the following observation: "Israel was not called to be an end in itself, but a means to an end; to be a servant of God through whom we have received the Sacred Scriptures as the Word of God, and Jesus Christ according to the flesh as the Saviour of the world. Jesus Christ and the church which is His body is the fulfillment, not an accidental afterthought, but the intended goal from the beginning; the fulfillment of the vocation of Abraham to be a blessing and of Israel to be a kingdom of priests and a holy nation" (*Backgrounds,* p. 152).

Dispensationalism assumes that God must restore Israel as a national theocracy and the ancient peoples of Edom, Moab, and Ammon also as independent nations in the future. The concept does not allow Jesus Christ and the New Testament to provide a new perspective for interpreting the Old Testament.

For Christians, the words of Christ and of the New Testament must be the ultimate guideline in matters of understanding the Old Testament prophecies with regard to their fulfillment in history. Not Israel but Christ is the real center and focus of the Holy Scriptures. But dispensationalists claim that "God has unconditionally promised a seed, a land, a king, a kingdom and a new heart to Israel. Lest God be a liar, these promises must be fulfilled" (J. Dwight Pentecost, "The Godly Remnant of the Tribulation Period," *Bibliotheca Sacra* CXVII [1959]: 133).

According to this line of reasoning, Israel is still God's chosen people, and the promises made to them were not conditional. Walvoord says that the only condition was that Abraham leave his homeland. "The covenant having been solemnly established, is now dependent upon the divine veracity for its fulfillment" (*The Abrahamic Covenant and Premillennialism,* p. 37, in Fuller, *Hermeneutics,* p. 245).

Dispensational theologians agree that if the promises were conditional, then the Jews would have forfeited their claim to Palestine. "Whether or not the Abrahamic promises were conditional or unconditional is an important question. If they were conditional on the Jews' faithfulness or goodness, we can assume the Jews have forfeited any claims to Palestine, for they have sinned repeatedly" (Epp, *Brief Outlines,* p. 75).

Were the promises conditional or unconditional? Let the inspired words be the judge. Looking at a few of the promises leaves no doubt on the subject.

"Keep and seek for all the commandments of the Lord your God: that ye may possess this good land, and leave it for an inheritance for your children forever" (1 Chronicles 28:8).

"Wherefore it shall come to pass, if ye hearken to these judgments, and keep, and do them, that the Lord thy God shall keep unto thee the covenant and the mercy which he sware unto thy fathers" (Deuteronomy 7:12).

"All the commandments which I command thee this day shall ye observe to do, that ye may live, and multiply, and go in and possess the land which the Lord sware unto your fathers" (Deuteronomy 8:1).

"And it shall be, if thou do at all forget the Lord thy God, and walk after other gods, and serve them, and worship them, I testify against you this day that ye shall surely perish" (verse 19).

"Ye shall therefore keep my statutes and my judgments, and shall not commit any of these abominations; neither any of your own nation . . . that the land spue not you out also, when ye defile it, as it spued out the nations that were before you" (Leviticus 18:26-28).

"Ye shall therefore keep all my statutes, and all my judgments, and do them: that the land, whither I bring you to dwell therein, spue you not out" (Leviticus 20:22).

This is just a sample of the promises made to Israel, showing that they were indeed conditional in nature.

According to the dispensational way of interpretation, it is unwise to apply the promises to Israel in any nonliteral sense. We must never use them for the church or spiritual Israel.

"There is not a single reference in the New Testament to

Israel which cannot be taken in its plain meaning. There is no justification based on usage in the New Testament to interpret the word Israel as ever including Gentiles" (John Walvoord, "Israel's Restoration," *Bibliotheca Sacra* CIII [1946]: 409).

Once again we call upon the Bible to test this claim.

"That the Gentiles should be fellowheirs, and of the same body, and partakers of his promise in Christ by the gospel" (Ephesians 3:6).

"For he is not a Jew, which is one outwardly; neither is that circumcision, which is outward in the flesh: but he is a Jew, which is one inwardly; and circumcision is that of the heart, in the spirit, and not in the letter; whose praise is not of men, but of God" (Romans 2:28, 29).

"There is neither Jew nor Greek, there is neither bond nor free, there is neither male nor female: for ye are all one in Christ Jesus. And if ye be Christ's, then are ye Abraham's seed, and heirs according to the promise" (Galatians 3:28, 29).

The New Testament equates the church, as the spiritual body of Christ, with the seed of Abraham. To accept these passages literally is to accept a spiritual Israel despite Ryrie's insistence that "whether the world likes it or not, the Jews are God's chosen people" (*The Bible and Tomorrow's News,* p. 69).

Referring to 1 Peter 2:9, he tells us that we cannot apply Israel's promises to the church. Yet the Holy Spirit does apply them to the church. Peter, inspired by the Holy Spirit, says to the church: "But ye are a chosen generation, a royal priesthood, an holy nation, a peculiar people; that ye should shew forth the praises of him who hath called you out of darkness into his marvellous light" (1 Peter 2:9).

Paul, even more explicitly in his letter to the Galatians, applies Old Testament prophecies of the kingdom in a spiritual manner to the believing Gentiles. "As many as walk according to this rule, peace be on them, and mercy, and upon the Israel of God" (Galatians 6:16).

His olive tree analogy clearly indicates this. "And if some of the branches be broken off, and thou, being a wild olive tree, wert graffed in among them, and with them partakest of the root and fatness of the olive tree" (Romans 11:17).

Can we expect spiritual fulfillments to the promises made to literal Israel? Paul says: "For all the promises of God in him are yea, and in him Amen, unto the glory of God by us" (2 Corinthians 1:20). That is, the Old Testament promises meet their fulfillment in Christ Himself.

The same God who inspired the Old Testament has inspired the New Testament. The New Testament is a continuation of the Old. We unlock the doors of the Old Testament with the key of the New. Jesus is the true interpretation of Old Testament promises. That is why He commanded: "Search the scriptures; for in them ye think ye have eternal life: and they are they which testify of me" (John 5:39). Jesus was saying to the Jews of His time, "You search the Scriptures because you think you have eternal life in them. But you forget that they testify of Me." The Old Testament Scriptures reveal Christ. You cannot accept the Scriptures of Christ and reject the Christ of the Scriptures.

Jesus told the disciples that the Temple in Jerusalem would be destroyed, that there would not be left "one stone upon another" (Matthew 24:2). He said nothing about it being a temporary condition, nothing about rebuilding the Temple. He wept over Jerusalem, saying: "O Jerusalem, Jerusalem, thou that killest the prophets, and stonest them which are sent unto thee, how often would I have gathered thy children together, even as a hen gathereth her chickens under her wings, and ye would not! Behold, your house is left unto you desolate" (Matthew 23:37, 38).

In this light we can understand Jesus' decisive words: "The kingdom of God shall be taken from you, and given to a nation bringing forth the fruits thereof" (Matthew 21:43).

Truly, the gathering of people from many nations to modern political Israel has been impressive. But an even greater gathering will take place in the near future, and the decisive point is not some hill or earthly city, not some race or territory or blood. It is a gathering of faith, something much more significant than anything that happened in 1948.

Of this gathering Jesus says: "And I, if I be lifted up from the earth, will draw all men unto me" (John 12:32).

The Old Testament book of Zechariah contains some of the promises to Israel. "And it shall come to pass in that day, that I will seek to destroy all the nations that come against Jerusalem" (Zechariah 12:9). History has seen a literal fulfillment of this prophecy. Many of the nations that have attacked Jerusalem have been destroyed. But that is just a small part of the prophecy. There exists so much more. To focus on a little piece of real estate in the Middle East is to miss the main part of the prophecy.

The next verse leads us into the important part of God's Word. "And I will pour upon the house of David, and upon the inhabitants of Jerusalem, the spirit of grace and of supplications: and they shall look upon me whom they have pierced, and they shall mourn for him, as one mourneth for his only son, and shall be in bitterness for him, as one that is in bitterness for his firstborn" (verse 10).

There is no doubt of whom the prophet is speaking! Zechariah 11:12 tells us that it was Someone who was sold for 30 pieces of silver.

To try to find a Christless meaning to these prophecies is to lose their significance completely. Israel is not the central theme of the Bible. Christ is!

"Who is this Jesus of Nazareth I have heard so much about?" a Jewish youth named Joseph once asked.

"A Jew of great talent," the boy's father replied, "but he pretended to be the Messiah, and the Jewish tribunal sentenced him to death."

"But why is Jerusalem destroyed and why are we in captivity?" his son continued.

"Because the Jews murdered the prophets," the father answered.

The young man began to ponder. "Perhaps He was a prophet too. Could it be that we have misunderstood His mission?"

Joseph was only 7 at the time. He questioned an elderly neighbor about the coming Messiah.

"Dear boy, I will tell you who the real Messiah was. He was Jesus of Nazareth. Go home and read the fifty-third chapter of Isaiah, and you will be convinced."

Joseph did just that, and when he grew up he became a great Christian missionary who proclaimed the gospel with mighty power. Joseph Wolff has been called "missionary to the world."

On the eve of each Independence Day in the nation of Israel, following the blasts of the trumpet, someone recites: "May it by thy will, O Jehovah our God and the God of our fathers, that as we have been granted the dawn of redemption, so may we be granted to hear the trumpet of Messiah."

It is a beautiful prayer, and the Bible says that someday soon the trumpet will indeed sound. Speaking of the last days of the history of our planet, Scripture declares: "In that day there shall be a fountain opened to the house of David and to the inhabitants of Jerusalem for sin and for uncleanness" (Zechariah 13:1).

That fountain is open now. John says: "If we confess our sins, he is faithful and just to forgive us our sins, and to cleanse us from all unrighteousness" (1 John 1:9).

It doesn't matter where you were born. That fountain is open to you now. "There is no difference between Jew and Gentile. You are all one in Christ" is the message of the New Testament Scriptures. It is the only salvation that the Bible offers.

Chapter 9

COUNTDOWN TO ANTICHRIST

Shawn Boonstra

You'd be surprised at who people have identified as the antichrist. Walk into any used book store and take a look at the bewildering array of recent candidates, ranging from Mikhail Gorbachev and Kurt Waldheim to Muammar Qaddafi and Ronald Reagan.

Ronald Reagan? Absolutely. Believe it or not, in some Christian circles he used to be a serious contender for the title. After all, his full name *is* Ronald Wilson Reagan, and each of those names has six letters—666! Furthermore, when an assassin shot him and Brady in 1981, Brady *almost* died, but his "deadly wound was healed"!

The suggestion now seems absurd, given that Reagan has passed from the world's spotlight. But that hasn't stopped speculation.

We find an almost endless list of contenders for the dubious honor of antichrist. Some Christian ministries seem to change their minds on an almost weekly basis. Tired of playing "pin the tail on the beast," some Christians have thrown up their hands in frustration. "Who can know for sure?" they ask.

If Bible prophecy is not being fulfilled in an unbroken chain of events throughout the course of history, and if the clock stopped at Calvary and will not start again until earth's final seven years (as dispensationalists claim), we really have no idea where we are. The clock could start again at any time. And so we are forced into a guessing game. Almost *anybody* could be the antichrist.

The Bible, however, does not deal with guessing games or prophetic uncertainty: "Blessed is he that readeth, and they that hear the words of this prophecy, and keep those things which are written therein: for the time is at hand" (Revelation 1:3).

"And he saith unto me, Seal not the sayings of the prophecy of this book: for the time is at hand" (Revelation 22:10).

As John opens the book of Revelation, he makes it clear that he wrote it to be understood. In fact, he pronounces a blessing on those who read it and do what it says. At the end of the book an angel instructs him not to seal what he wrote, "for the time is at hand." The events that John witnessed in prophetic vision were to begin their fulfillment immediately.[1]

Most scholars date the book of Revelation to the end of the first century, more than 60 years *after* the events at Calvary. If the prophetic clock stopped at the Crucifixion and if the prophets could not see the events between Calvary and the final seven years of history, why would the angel bother to tell John that the time was "at hand"? After all, according to dispensationalists, John was already living in the dark, uncharted period of the "dispensation of grace." Nothing would be "at hand" for almost 2,000 years.

The Bible, however, knows no gap in prophetic history. It gives us an uninterrupted schedule of events from the days of the prophets until Jesus returns. Daniel 7, building on the world empire prophecy of Daniel 2, offers a clear example of an unbroken prophetic time line for Planet Earth. It provides a clear itinerary from Daniel's time to the days of the "little horn" power, which turns out to be the same thing as the antichrist "beast" power of Revelation 13. Daniel, in effect, gives us a countdown to antichrist.

"Daniel spake and said, I saw in my vision by night, and, behold, the four winds of the heaven strove upon the great sea. And four great beasts came up from the sea, diverse one from another" (Daniel 7:2, 3).[2]

When we compare Daniel's dream with the vision John recounts in Revelation 13, the parallels are astonishing. "And I stood upon the sand of the sea, and saw a beast rise up out of the sea, having seven heads and ten horns, and upon his horns ten crowns, and upon his heads the name of blasphemy. And the beast which I saw was like unto a leopard, and his feet were as the feet of a bear, and his mouth as the mouth of a lion: and the dragon gave him his power, and his seat, and great authority" (Revelation 13:1, 2).

Both Daniel and John saw something crawl up out of the water. In Bible prophecy, water represents "peoples, and multitudes, and nations, and tongues" (Revelation 17:15) or the nations of earth. Although both visions describe beasts coming out of water, though, we do find a key difference between them. Daniel saw four separate beasts emerge from the water one at a time, while John observed only one conglomerate beast made up of parts of the beasts that Daniel witnessed.

The difference is significant. Daniel's vision gives us a progression of empires leading up to the time of the antichrist "little horn" power, thus revealing the beasts one at a time. John's vision in Revelation 13 is not a broad time line but is primarily about the antichrist itself, so he portrays it as a composite of all the empires that led up to its appearance.

Daniel 7 is the indispensable key to understanding the beast power of Revelation 13 and provides us a stunning panorama from Daniel's day through to the antichrist and the final judgment. Each of the beasts that Daniel watched climb out of the water represents a dominant political kingdom rising from among the nations of earth. "These great beasts, which are four, are four kings, which shall arise out of the earth" (Daniel 7:17). "Thus he said, The fourth beast shall be the fourth kingdom upon earth" (verse 23).

We do not need to speculate about the symbols of Bible prophecy. The Bible is its own best interpreter and will generally explain itself. A "beast" or animal in Bible prophecy represents a *kingdom,* an important clue to understanding what the "beast" of Revelation 13 represents. Certain modern Bible expositors have portrayed the beast of Revelation 13 as a single individual living at the close of earth's history. The biblical symbol of a beast, however, does not depict an individual but political powers, generally "kingdoms"—dominions ruled over by someone called "king."

The apostle Paul makes it crystal clear that antichrist cannot possibly be an individual, whether present or future. "Let no man deceive you by any means: for that day shall not come, except there come a falling away first, and that man of sin be revealed, the son of perdition; who opposeth and exalteth himself above all that is called God, or that is worshipped; so that he as God sitteth in the temple of God, shewing himself that he is God. . . . For the mystery of iniquity doth already work: only he who now letteth will let, until he be taken out of the way. And then shall that Wicked be revealed, whom the Lord shall consume with the spirit of his mouth, and shall destroy with the brightness of his coming" (2 Thessalonians 2:3-8).

Did you catch what he said here? Paul wrote that the "mystery of iniquity" was already at work in his day. He said that something was "letting" it—an old-fashioned English term (the King James Version was translated in 1611) meaning that something was holding it in check. The clear implication is that once the hindrance disappeared, "that Wicked" would be revealed and continue until the second coming of Christ.

Think about it. "Antichrist" cannot refer to a single individual. No human being could live from Paul's day until Jesus returns. Clearly, then, antichrist is not a single individual. This leaves us with the option that it refers to a *power,* an organizational system, which is why John portrays it as a *beast.* It is the successor to Daniel's earthly political dominions or kingdoms. (We shall be using the words "dominion," "kingdom," and "empire" interchangeably for human political governments.)

Daniel continues to describe the vision by talking about one beast/empire at a time. "The first was like a lion, and had eagle's wings: I beheld till the wings thereof were plucked, and it was lifted up from the earth, and made stand upon the feet as a man, and a man's heart was given to it. And behold another beast, a second, like to a bear, and it raised up itself on one side, and it had three ribs in the mouth of it between the teeth of it: and they said thus unto it, Arise, devour much flesh. After this I beheld, and lo another, like a leopard, which had upon the back of it four wings of a fowl; the beast had also four heads; and dominion was given to it. After this I saw in the night visions, and behold a fourth beast, dreadful and terrible, and strong exceedingly; and it had great iron teeth: it devoured and brake in pieces, and stamped the residue with the feet of it: and it was diverse from all the beasts that were before it; and it had ten horns" (Daniel 7:4-7).

Daniel describes a lion, a bear, a leopard, and a terrible beast like something out of a horror movie. Some modern expositors, understanding that in biblical prophecy an animal represents nations or political powers, take the beasts of Bible prophecy out of their original context and transplant them into the framework of our modern world. For example, because popular culture has come to identify a bear with Russia in our day, some assume that's what the Bible was talking about. But this is a serious mistake. The Bible must interpret itself, and the symbols must be understood in the context of the ancient Near East in which they were first introduced.

What, then, are the four kingdoms of Daniel's vision? The answer is important, because the parade of beasts give us a countdown to antichrist, the "little horn" power found later in the vision.

The Lion With Eagle's Wings—The lion was a well-known symbol for the neo-Babylonian Empire in Daniel's day. To this day when archaeologists explore the ruins of Babylon, they find images of lions, sometimes with eagle's wings. The book of Jeremiah repeatedly refers to the Babylonians as a lion: "The lion is come up from his thicket, and the destroyer of the Gentiles is on his way; he is gone forth from his place to make thy land desolate; and thy cities shall be laid waste, without an inhabitant" (Jeremiah 4:7).

Eagles and their wings served as biblical symbols for speed. For example, the same passage in Jeremiah compares the horses of Babylon to eagles: "Behold, he shall come up as clouds, and his chariots shall be as a whirlwind: his horses are swifter than eagles" (verse 13).

The prophet Habakkuk described the Babylonian armies in much the same language: "Their horses also are swifter than the leopards, and are more fierce than the evening wolves: and their horsemen shall spread themselves, and their horsemen shall come from far; they shall fly as the eagle that hasteth to eat" (Habakkuk 1:8).

The lion with eagle's wings was a fitting symbol of Babylon. Its armies brought swift and terrible punishment upon much of the ancient Near East. The neo-Babylonian juggernaut rose to prominence with King Nebuchadnezzar in 605 B.C. and dominated much of the Middle East until 539 B.C., when the armies of the Medes and the Persians entered the fortified city of Babylon.

The Bear With One Elevated Side—The second animal in Daniel's vision was a bear that had one shoulder higher than the other. It also had three ribs in its mouth. The Medes and the Persians sacked the city of Babylon in 539 B.C., on the very night that Belshazzar hosted the blasphemous drunken feast described in Daniel 5.

The Medo-Persian Empire was a coalition government. It was not, however, an evenly balanced coalition. The Persians quickly overshadowed the Medes, becoming the dominant party, which is why the vision in Daniel 7:5 portrays the bear as "raised up . . . on one side." It was unbalanced. Daniel 8 described (and actually *named*) the Medo-Persian regime as a ram with two unevenly sized horns.

Bears are nowhere near as nimble and graceful as lions, even though they can be ferocious. Daniel 2, in fact, distinctly refers to the Medo-Persian Empire as "inferior" to the Babylonian (verse 39), yet it managed to overthrow Babylon.

At the time of its collapse, the neo-Babylonian Empire consisted of three principal provinces. The Medes and Persians overthrew each province, and thus the vision depicts the bear with three ribs in its mouth.

The fall of Babylon to the Medo-Persian forces is one of the major themes woven through Bible prophecy. (Revelation 16, for example, symbolically uses the events of the collapse of the empire.) Cyrus the Great struck upon an ingenious plan to capture the heavily fortified city. The Euphrates River ran right through the heart of the city, flowing in a channel under the walls. According to the ancient historian Herodotus, Cyrus's general sent his men upstream to divert the river. The water level dropped enough to provide a virtual highway under the city walls and into the city proper.

Once inside, they had only one obstacle to overcome: the gates in the walls along the riverbed. Usually they were locked and guarded at all times, but on the night that Babylon fell, everyone was drunk and the gates had been left open. The invaders captured the city with hardly a fight. Sixteen days later King Cyrus himself triumphantly marched into Babylon.

The downfall of Babylon exactly fulfilled a Bible prophecy given more than 100 years before Cyrus's birth: "That saith to the deep, Be dry, and I will dry up thy rivers. . . . Thus saith the Lord to his anointed, to Cyrus, whose right hand I have holden, to subdue nations before him; and I will loose the loins of kings, to open before him the two leaved gates; and the gates shall not be shut" (Isaiah 44:27–45:2).

The Leopard With Four Wings—The expansion of the Persian kingdom put it in contact with the Greek cities of Asia, resulting in a series of struggles between Greece and Persia. In 331 B.C. a vast army of Persians fell victim to the armies of the famous Macedonian, Alexander the Great. It was one of the most decisive battles of history, signaling the end of the Persian Empire and paving the way for the spread of Hellenistic civilization throughout much of the world.

The Bible depicts the Macedonian (Greek) Empire as a leopard, a symbol of speed in Habakkuk 1:8. Whereas the Babylonian lion had only two wings to indicate its speed, the Greek leopard had four, representing even greater speed. The world had never seen an army as swift as Alexander's. It managed to conquer 20 million subjects spread out over 2 million square miles in less than 10 years—all before Alexander turned 32.

The four-winged leopard was an apt symbol. Once Alexander reached India, he brokenheartedly assumed that he had no more worlds to conquer, and he marched his army back to the ruined city of Babylon. There in 323 B.C. he suddenly died of a fever, which some believe had been brought on or at least exacerbated by his lifestyle. Some have speculated that although Alexander the Great had conquered much of the world, he couldn't conquer his own passions.

A brief struggle for control of the Greek Empire followed his death. Eventually the realm fell under the control of four of Alexander's generals: Cassander, Lysimachus, Ptolemy, and Seleucus. The divided empire remained under the leadership of these men and their families for many years. This is why the vision depicts the leopard as having four heads instead of one—an accurate description of the divided empire that had once been so powerful.

The Dreadful and Terrible Beast—The fourth beast in Daniel's vision, an iron-toothed monstrosity, was unlike anything he had ever seen. He could only describe it as "dreadful and terrible" as it overwhelmed everything around it.

In the year 168 B.C. the Roman consul Æmilius Paulus crushed the Macedonian army on the field of Pydna. In the words of the historian Philip Van Ness Meyers: "The short but great part which Macedonia as an independent state had played in history was ended. She now drops below the historical horizon" (*General History,* p. 242).

The Roman armies were unlike anything the world had ever seen. Almost nothing could survive a crushing Roman assault. Her iron teeth (remember the iron legs of the image in Daniel 2, which also represented the Roman Empire?) devoured most of the Mediterranean world. Of the four empires with their military machines mentioned in the book of Daniel, it is still the best remembered.

The Ten Horns—The Roman Empire eventually crumbled as it indulged itself in excesses and came under the onslaughts of the barbarian tribes of Europe. After a series of impotent puppet kings, a child found himself placed on the Roman throne. The Heruli, a small Germanic tribe under the direction of Odoacer, removed the child emperor from the throne in A.D. 476, and the Roman Empire in the West was dead. (The Eastern Roman Empire continued alive and well for many more centuries.)

Individual European kingdoms, each of them a barbaric tribe, replaced the Western segment.

• Alemanni (Germans)	• Anglo-Saxons (English)
• Visigoths (Spaniards)	• Lombards (Italians)
• Franks (French)	• Ostrogoths (extinct)
• Suevi (Portuguese)	• Vandals (extinct)
• Burgundians (Swiss)	• Heruli (extinct)

Note the number of them—10.

Daniel's vision accurately showed these 10 horns coming up out of the head of the Roman Empire. We have no doubt about what a horn represents, since Daniel explains it very clearly: "And the ten horns out of this kingdom are ten kings that shall arise" (Daniel 7:24).

Horns, like animals, in Scripture symbolize power, especially political power. Ancient Near Eastern iconography sometimes depicts a king with horns sprouting from his head. The imagery of a horn, however, better fits the concept of authority rather than a portrayal of a single individual, which is critical to a clear understanding of the issues presented in Revelation 13.

John described the antichrist power as a "beast," whereas Daniel calls it a "little horn." In fact, it's the next thing that Daniel saw: "I considered the horns, and, behold, there came up among them another little horn, before whom there were three of the first horns plucked up by the roots: and, behold, in this horn were eyes like the eyes of man, and a mouth speaking great things" (Daniel 7:8).

As it turns out, this little horn behaves just like the antichrist beast of Revelation 13, making it relatively easy to conclude that Daniel 7 and Revelation 13 depict the same power. What power? The Bible leaves little room for doubt.

---

[1] I am aware, of course, that an angel told Daniel to "seal" his book until the time of the end. That does not imply, however, a gap in Daniel's prophecies. It merely means that it would not be understood clearly until the time of the end, when "knowledge" would be "increased" (Daniel 12:4).

[2] Do not be misled by the English word "beast." The word in today's language can have the connotation of an uncontrollable creature—a very dangerous being, as in "a wild beast" or "he was a beast of a man." The Hebrew word used in Daniel simply meant a living thing—any animal, even sometimes a human being. It did not necessarily have ominous or scary overtones.

Chapter 10

THE LITTLE HORN

Shawn Boonstra

Until the speculations of Ribera and Bellarmine and their modern dispensationalist followers, most Christians had little doubt as to what the "little horn" of Daniel 7 represented. The Protestant Reformers, as they studied prophetic passages such as Daniel 7 and Revelation 13, understood that antichrist would appear in the regular course of history. The notion of a prophetic "gap" of hundreds or thousands of years was completely unheard of.

Modern confusion on the subject has arisen because of the Counter-Reformation. New ideas based on speculation rather than solid Bible evidence have been thrust upon an unsuspecting Christendom, resulting in the bewilderment of Christians everywhere.

Some have attempted to say that the blame for confusion lies with the Bible itself, because what it portrays is simply too "deep" or "mysterious" for the average person to understand. Nothing could be further from the truth. The Bible offers enough evidence to help inquirers identify the antichrist little horn power. Let's examine the evidence.

1. The little horn is in the Mediterranean world. Daniel 7:8 suggests that the little horn power came up *among* the political entities—the 10 horns—that divided up the Western Roman Empire. (The narrative of events appears to ignore the Eastern

THE RETURN

Roman Empire, which continued to prosper for many more centuries following A.D. 476 when the western part of the Roman Empire disintegrated.) Although Daniel described it as a *little* horn, smaller than the others, it ends up being the most prominent. Daniel tells us that although it may have been "little," it was "more stout than his fellows" (verse 20).[1] We can, therefore, safely deduce that the little horn is a small—but influential—European power.

2. The little horn had to appear after A.D. 476. This is the only logical possibility, since Daniel tells us that it arose among the 10 horns. The 10 horns developed out of the Roman Empire, which collapsed in A.D. 476.

3. The little horn uprooted three of the 10 horns (Daniel 7:8, 20, 24). We conclude from this that three of the barbarian tribes that contributed to Rome's demise would themselves disappear. You will notice, in the table of barbarian nations given in the previous chapter, that three of them are now extinct—the Heruli, the Vandals, and the Ostrogoths.

4. It is different from other kingdoms. Daniel 7:24 says of the little horn power that "he shall be diverse from the first." The word "diverse" is simply an archaic way of saying "different." Something unusual about this "little" but "more stout" power makes it completely different from other kingdoms.

5. It has a mouth that speaks "great words," probably blasphemies. Daniel 7:25 tells us that "he shall speak great words against the most High." Revelation 13:5 echoes this: "There was given unto him a mouth speaking great things." Furthermore, Revelation 13:5 explains the expression "great things" by adding a synonym—"blasphemies."

What is blasphemy? The word appears much more frequently in the New Testament than in the Old Testament.[2] The New Testament helps us define it: "The Jews answered him, saying, For a good work we stone thee not; but for blasphemy; and because that thou, being a man, makest thyself God" (John 10:33).

The context of their criticism of Jesus makes it quite clear that blasphemy can involve trying to place oneself on par with God. It expands on this concept to include claiming divine attributes. Notice this expansion of the same idea: "But there were certain of the scribes sitting there, and reasoning in their hearts, Why doth this man thus speak blasphemies? who can forgive sins but God only?" (Mark 2:6, 7).

According to the Bible, then, "speaking blasphemy" can involve the claim to be equal to God or to be able to do something that only God can do, such as forgive sins.

6. It is a persecuting power. Daniel 7:25 tells us that the new power would "wear out the saints." John the revelator describes the same thing: "It was given unto him to make war with the saints, and to overcome them: and power was given him over all kindreds, and tongues, and nations" (Revelation 13:7). The entity persecutes those who disagree with it or do not submit to its authority.

7. It would think to "change times and laws" (Daniel 7:25). More about this later, but if God's laws were what it tried to change, then one can see that this could well be another aspect of blasphemy on the part of the little horn power.

8. It would rule supreme for a time, times, and the dividing of time (Daniel 7:25). A period of time prominent in Bible prophecy, Scripture describes it different ways. Revelation 12:14 calls it "a time, and times, and half a time." Revelation 12:6 refers to it as 1,260 days, and Revelation 13:5 calls it "forty and two months."

These periods of time are all identical. A "time" is a code word for year, which in round figures consisted of 360 days. A "time, times, and dividing of time" is simply a year, two years (biblical Hebrew had a word ending that meant "two" and another word ending that meant plural—more than two), and half a year, for a total of 1,260 days. Forty-two months, each made up of 30 days, also totals 1,260 days.

In Bible prophecy, the words "day" and "days" have symbolic meaning. Elsewhere in the Bible a "day" generally refers to a literal 24-hour period of time, as in the Creation account. In prophecy, however, a day represents a year. Good examples of a "day for a year" appear in Ezekiel 4:6 and Numbers 14:34.[3] Most every serious Bible scholar recognizes this fact when it comes to the Messianic prophecy of Daniel 9. The principle also applies here.

The Bible thus reveals that the "little horn" power would hold sway for 1,260 literal years.

9. It is identified by the number 666 (Revelation 13:18).

Once you line up all of the clues given in Scripture, it is not hard to see why the Reformers and so many other Bible students throughout history came to the conclusion that they did. Only one power in earth's history fits all nine identifying points. Many of the modern candidates for antichrist might vaguely resemble two or three characteristics, but not all nine. The only thing that counts is an exact match—and the only institution that matches every last point is the church-state entity often called the papal system.

We need to be careful, however, to establish what the Bible is *not* identifying. It is not pointing to individuals within Christianity or Roman Catholicism. Thus it has in mind a religiopolitical *power, not a person.* Some people become confused on this point and have attempted to name individual popes as antichrist in an effort to reconcile dispensationalist thinking with the Bible's clear description of the beast/little horn power.

Noah Hutchings, for instance, of the Southwest Radio Church, attempted in 1984 to identify Pope John Paul II as *the* antichrist because of the failed attempt on his life. "In Pope John Paul II we see a man who is rising in international stature, a man who will be increasingly called upon to bring peace to a troubled world. His recovery from a deadly wound directed world attention and admiration to his personage, and he, like those before him, would seemingly like to establish his authority over the Holy Hill of Zion" (in William M. Alnor, *Soothsayers of the Second Advent,* p. 22).

By now it should be clear to all readers that he and others are wrong. The beast of Revelation 13 is *not* an individual pope. The biblical symbols point to an *institution*—the papal church-state as a powerful entity. Individual popes have been responsible for the *record* of the Roman Church, but they do not in and of themselves make up the antichrist power. They are merely components of it. As clearly stated previously, Bible prophecy uses the symbols of horns and animals to specify kingdoms and political entities, not individuals.

Do all the pieces really fit Rome? Let's review all nine identifying points to see how they fit.

1. The little horn is in the Mediterranean world. There can be no doubt about this one. The Papacy appeared out of the divided ruins of the Western Roman Empire. The historian Philip Van Ness Meyers says: "Another consequence of the fall of the Roman power in the West was the development of the Papacy. In the absence of an emperor in the West the popes rapidly gained influence and power, and soon built up an ecclesiastical empire that in some respects took the place of the old Empire and carried on its civilizing work" (*General History,* p. 316).

The Christian church-state not only appeared among the 10 barbarian tribes of Europe as the Bible predicted, but it also soon ascended to a position of preeminence among them, becoming "more stout"—more prominent—than the others despite Rome's small geographical size.

2. The little horn had to appear after A.D. 476. This is also true. When Justinian took the throne in Constantinople in A.D. 527, one of his first orders of business was to reorganize what remained of the Roman Empire. Concerned about overall unity, he declared the bishop of Rome to be the "head of all the holy churches" (S. P. Scott, *A.M., Corpus Juris Civilis [The Civil Law, the Code of Justinian],* vol. 12, pp. 9-12).

Justinian's famous code of laws, ratified by A.D. 533, thus made the bishop of Rome the formal head of Christianity—at least on paper. Some of the barbarian tribes of Europe embraced the idea. The Franks had already declared themselves loyal to Rome when their king, Clovis, converted to the Roman Catholic faith some years earlier and became the protector and patron of Christian church-state leadership.

But certain tribes that ascribed to the teachings of a heretic priest named Arius stood in the way of Justinian's wishes. They refused to acknowledge the supremacy of the bishop of Rome. The church/Roman armies crushed the last of these tribes in A.D. 538, thereby establishing the preeminence of the Papacy.

3. The little horn uprooted three of the 10 horns (Daniel 7:8, 20, 24). The three barbarian Arian tribes that stood in the way of the realization of Justinian's decree were the Heruli, the

Vandals, and the Ostrogoths. Their refusal to recognize the bishop of Rome as the "head of all the holy churches" threatened the latter's power.

In A.D. 493 the armies of Theodoric, under a commission from Rome, destroyed the Heruli (Edward Gibbon, *Decline and Fall of the Roman Empire,* chaps. 39, 40). Their defeat was so resounding that today the Heruli no longer exist.

In A.D. 534, at the request of Justinian, General Belisarius destroyed the Vandals. It was part of an effort to crush the threat they represented to the Christian leadership in the West. As a nation, the Vandals ceased to exist.

So two horns were uprooted, leaving only one more. Once Belisarius had wiped out the Vandals, he turned his attention to the Ostrogoths and drove them away from Rome. In A.D. 537 they returned and laid siege to the city. Justinian sent in more forces, and during the next year so completely defeated the Ostrogoths that they never again posed a threat to Rome. By 554 they had vanished off the Mediterranean map.

That made A.D. 538 a landmark year, because the powers conferred upon the bishop of Rome by Justinian became a reality. The three potentially dangerous horn powers had been removed, and the church leadership began enjoying supremacy over what had once been the Western Roman Empire.

4. It is different from other kingdoms. What makes the Papacy different from other kingdoms is its *religio*political nature. Not only is the Vatican a religious power, but it is also a political one. Its laws are not dictated by monarchs or politicians, but rather by the clergy. The Papacy exemplifies the marriage of the Christian church to the state like no other institution in human history. And perhaps that is the crux of the issue. Whereas it is a truism that absolute power corrupts absolutely, the combination of religious and political power is even more a problem, because it affords even greater opportunities to misuse authority by cloaking it with spiritual overtones and divine sanction.

5. It has a mouth that speaks "great words," probably blasphemies. As we have seen already, the Bible defines "blasphemy" as claiming to be God or to have attributes of God, such as the power to forgive sin. Without question the papal church-state has exerted such claims. The prestigious *Catholic Encyclopedia* has described Ferraris's ecclesiastical dictionary as a "veritable encyclopedia of religious knowledge" and a "precious mine of information."

Notice how Ferraris describes the institution of the Papacy: **"Pope, exaltation of:** The pope is so great dignity and so exalted that he is not a mere man, but as it were God, and the vicar of God.

"The pope is of such lofty and supreme dignity that, properly speaking, he has not been established in any rank of dignity, but rather has been placed upon the summit of all ranks of dignities.

"The pope is called holy because he is rightfully presumed to be such. . . . He is likewise the Divine monarch and supreme emperor and King of Kings.

"Hence the pope is crowned with a triple crown, as king of heaven and of earth and of the lower regions.

"Moreover, the superiority and the power of the Roman pontiff by no means pertain only to heavenly things, to earthly things and to things under the earth, but are even over angels, than whom he is greater. . . .

"For he is of so great dignity and power that he forms one and the same tribunal with Christ. So that whatever the pope does, seems to proceed from the mouth of God. . . .

"The pope is as it were God on earth, sole sovereign of the faithful of Christ, chief king of kings, having plenitude of power" (Lucius Ferraris, "Papa," in *Prompta Bibliotheca Canonica, Juridica, Moralis, Theologica, Necnon Ascetica, Polemica, Rubricistica, Historica* [1858] vol. 5).

It is no secret that the bishops of Rome have often been referred to as vicars of Christ, a phrase that literally means that he is thought to stand in the place of Christ. Some might argue that the title simply means that the pope is a *representative* of Christ. But an article in the *Catholic National*, July 1895, declared: "The pope is not only the representative of Jesus Christ, but he is Jesus Christ, Himself, hidden under the veil of flesh."

At the fourth session of the Fifth Lateran Council of 1512, Christopher Marcellus addressed the pope this way, much to the approbation of his peers: "For thou art the shepherd, thou art the physician, thou art the governor, thou art the husbandman; finally, thou art another God on earth."

Unfortunately, we have no record of any pope refusing such a designation. In reality, popes have even advanced such declarations themselves, as did Pope Leo XIII: "We hold upon this earth the place of God Almighty" (encyclical letter of June 20, 1894).

Not only has the Papacy made claims to equality with God,[4] but it sees itself as having God's power to forgive sins. Some have argued that the Roman Catholic priest merely informs penitents that God has forgiven their sins, but Catholic teaching includes more than that: "The priest does really and truly forgive sins in virtue of the power given to him by Christ" (Joseph DeHarbe, *Catechism of the Catholic Religion,* p. 279).

Some years ago Roman Catholic writer Michael Muller published a book describing the various powers of the Catholic priest. Here's what he said about Rome's claim to forgive sinners. "Seek where you will, through heaven and earth, and you will find but one created being who can forgive the sinner, who can free him from the chains of hell. That extraordinary being is the priest, the Catholic priest. Yes, beloved brethren, the priest not only declares that the sinner is forgiven, but he really forgives him. The priest raises his hand, he pronounces the world of absolution, and in an instant, quick as a flash of light the chains of hell are burst asunder, and the sinner becomes a child of God. So great is the power of the priest that the judgments of heaven itself are subject to his decision" (*The Catholic Priest,* pp. 78, 79).

We can only interpret such a claim as blasphemy. The Bible is clear that only one mediator exists between God and humanity—Jesus Christ (1 Timothy 2:5). The papal church-state system has sought to assume Christ's authority to forgive sins, a power that according to the Bible only God Himself rightfully possesses.

6. It is a persecuting power. This point hardly needs comment. Countless thousands perished because of matters of conscience during medieval times, a fact that the Roman Catholic Church acknowledges. Some authorities estimate the death toll to be 50 million people while others have guessed much higher.

Some of the most notable periods of papal persecution include the pontificate of Innocent III (1198-1216) and the Spanish Inquisition, during which many lost their lives. The Magdeburg Massacre and the Massacre of St. Bartholomew stand out as other notable incidents during which religious leaders participated in the deaths of thousands. After the St. Bartholomew Massacre, during an "open season" declared on Huguenots (estimates of deaths vary from 2,000 to 70,000), Rome minted commemorative medals to congratulate the pope on a job well done. And Pope Gregory XIII himself celebrated with a *Te Deum* in Rome.

The *Western Watchman,* a Catholic publication, declared: "The church has persecuted. Only a tyro in church history will deny that" (*Western Watchman,* December 23, 1908).

7. It would think to "change times and laws" (Daniel 7:25). Those who have carefully compared the Ten Commandments as listed in the Bible to those listed in Catholic catechisms will notice something unusual. The second commandment, which forbids the use of images for worship, is entirely missing from the catechism, and the tenth commandment, forbidding covetousness, has been split in two in order to make a full 10 commandments.

Bishop Louis LaRavoire Morrow explains: "The Catholic system is based on the Hebrew text, and principally on the enumeration made by St. Augustine; it was adopted by the Council of Trent. By it, the first commandment contains everything relating to false worship and false gods. The tenfold division is safeguarded by dividing the last precept regarding desire into one relating to sins of the flesh, and another referring to sins against property, just as *acts* against purity are forbidden separately from acts against property.

"The English Protestant enumeration is based on Origen and others. By it the worship of graven images is numbered as the Second Commandment, and all the succeeding commandments thereby are advanced one over the Catholic enumeration. To safeguard the tenfold division, the last two commandments are grouped together as the Tenth" (*My Catholic Faith: A Manual of Religion,* p. 195).

During the Reformation, Christians persistently pointed out that the Roman Church ignored the second commandment through the veneration of images in the church. As a result, the Counter-Reformation Council of Trent permanently adopted a questionable system of numbering the Ten Commandments that eliminated the second.

Bishop Morrow argues that Protestants number their commandments according to a system devised by Origen, who did most of his work in the third century. In *Antiquities of the Jews,* however, Josephus (who lived in the first century, during the time the New Testament was written) gives us the common understanding of the Ten Commandments back in the days of Christ: "The first commandment teaches us, That there is but one God, and that we ought to worship him only; the second commands us not to make the image of any living creature to worship it; the third, That we must not swear by God in a false matter; the fourth, That we must keep the seventh day, by resting from all sorts of work; the fifth, That we must honour our parents; the sixth, That we must abstain from murder; the seventh, That we must not commit adultery; the eighth, That we must not be guilty of theft; the ninth, That we must not bear false witness; the tenth, That we must not admit of the desire of any thing that is another's" (*Antiquities of the Jews,* Book III, Chap. V, in William Whiston, trans., *The Complete Works of Josephus,* pp. 70, 71).

In attempting to explain Protestant numbering by attributing it to "Origen and others," representatives of the papal system sought to present their numbering as a viable alternative. It was not entrenched until many years after the close of the Christian canon, however.

Still, Rome feels that it has the authority to make such changes, as we see in the following document: **"The Pope:** The pope is of so great authority and power that he can modify, change, or interpret even divine laws. The pope can modify divine law, since his power is not of man, but of God, and he acts as viceregent of God upon earth with most ample power of binding and loosing his sheep" (Lucius Ferraris, "Papa," art. 2, in *Prompta Bibliotheca,* col. 1823).

Again we must return to our discussion of what constitutes blasphemy. Rome teaches that the Papacy is above even God's law. At the Council of Trent, Gaspare de Posso, the archbishop of Reggio, in a speech made on January 18, 1562, declared: "The authority of the church is illustrated most clearly by the Scriptures; for while on one hand she [the church] recommends them, declares them to be divine, [and] offers them to us to be read, . . . on the other hand, the legal precepts in the Scriptures taught by the Lord have ceased by virtue of the same authority [the church]. The Sabbath, the most glorious day in the law, has been changed into the Lord's day. . . . These and other similar matters have not ceased by virtue of Christ's teaching (for He says He has come to fulfill the law, not to destroy it), but they have been changed by the authority of the church" (J. D. Mansi, ed., *Sacrorum Conciliorum,* 33:529, 530, in C. Mervyn Maxwell, *God Cares,* vol. 1, p. 128).

Without question the Papacy, especially during the Middle Ages, more than any other institution in the history of Christianity, has made deliberate attempts to change God's law—and times.

8. It would rule supreme for a time, times, and the dividing of time (Daniel 7:25). When Western church leadership eliminated the threat posed by the Ostrogoths in A.D. 538, the decree of Justinian making the bishop of Rome the "head of all the holy churches" became a reality. Almost all of Christendom gathered under the umbrella of the pope—and it stayed there for a long, long time.[5]

The Protestant Reformation signaled the beginning of the end for the centralized authority of the Papacy as one group after another severed its ties with Rome, yet the political power of the papal church-state system survived for many years after Luther nailed his 95 theses to the church door in Wittenberg.

In 1798, however, exactly 1,260 years after the establishment of the Papacy as the supreme authority over the churches in the former Western Roman Empire, something significant happened. France (the European tribe that was the first to endorse and embrace the Roman Catholic faith) began to feel the effects of the French Revolution. Its leaders generally discarded religion and sought to enthrone the Goddess of Reason in place of Christ.

In February of 1798 General Alexander Berthier, under orders from Napoleon, arrested Pope Pius VI as he celebrated the anniversary of his coronation in the Sistine Chapel. The French troops dethroned and imprisoned the pope. He died in exile. The French confiscated his private library, and all of his subjects came under military control (L. E. Froom, *Prophetic Faith,* vol. 2, p. 753). A republic was declared.

One historical writer says of that day: "The papacy was extinct: not a vestige of its existence remained; and among all the Roman Catholic powers not a finger was stirred" (G. Trevor, *Rome From the Fall of the Western Empire,* p. 440, in Froom, vol. 3, p. 327).

9. It is identified by the number 666 (Revelation 13:18). In the next chapter we'll spend some time examining this number.

---

[1] "Stout" is one of those old words that centuries ago had many meanings. It does not necessarily mean "fatter" or "heavier." *The Oxford English Dictionary* enumerates such meanings as "formidable," "menacing," "terrible in appearance," "proud," "stately," "severe," "valiant," "vigorous," "hardy," "strenuous," "firm in resolve," "stubborn," "rebellious," "strong," among other terms. The Hebrew literally means "its visibility was greater." The idea is that although this horn was "little" in size, it was very prominent. Perhaps the gist here is something of a warning: "Don't let its size fool you."

[2] The English word "blaspheme" is a Greek loan word and is almost a literal transliteration of the Greek. The word comes from two roots: one means "harsh," and the other means "utterance." In secular Greek it referred to various types of abusive language, for example, mockery. Ancient Grecians also gave the term a religious meaning—that of mistaking the true nature of the gods or doubting their power. The Bible typically uses it in reference to God and employs it for desecrating His name, denying His power, speaking in an ungodly manner, and dishonoring Him. In other words, it meant irreverent speech against God.

[3] Notice that in Daniel 4:23-25 the prophet told Nebuchadnezzar that he would lose his sanity for seven "times," or years.

[4] Compare this with Scripture: "Who opposeth and exalteth himself above all that is called God, or that is worshipped; so that he as God sitteth in the temple of God, shewing himself that he is God" (2 Thessalonians 2:4).

[5] I refer to "almost all" because various groups throughout history, such as the Waldensians and others, continued to resist the church's centralized authority. For the most part, however, the European nations all came under the jurisdiction of Rome.

Chapter 11

THE NUMBER OF THE BEAST—666

Shawn Boonstra

I remember going to the grocery store one afternoon to pick up a couple of items for my wife. When the cashier rang them up, the total came to $6.66. A look of horror washed over her face. "Boy," she said, "are you sure you wouldn't like to buy something else?"

"Why would I do that?" I asked.

"Just look at your total. It's the number of the beast!"

At first I thought she must be kidding, but the expression on her face told me that she was only *half* kidding. Something about the number 666 on her till really disturbed her. Of course, she knew that I wasn't out buying groceries for the antichrist, but the ominous appearance of the number on her cash register gave her pause for somber thought. Was it a bad omen?

It has given *many* Christians pause for somber thought. Most profess to have no idea who or what the number actually represents, and many simply treat it as a harbinger of evil. The superstition maintains that wherever it shows up, something bad is bound to happen.

What does this mysterious number actually mean? In modern North American Christianity, saturated with dispensationalist thinking, the number is a big question mark. Such Christians see no need to look for it in history, because antichrist has not yet appeared. It could represent just about anybody or anything—in the future.

One of the more popular theories circulating in evangelical Christianity revolves around the idea that antichrist is a big supercomputer (often located in Belgium) nicknamed "The Beast." Allegedly it tracks the financial transactions of everybody on our planet. Supposedly the self-programming creation of the architects of the European Common Market, it was built to provide every person on earth with a registration number, thereby giving them the "mark of the beast." Some accounts I have seen indicate that the address that houses the evil machine is 666 or that the machine itself prominently displays the number.

Under close scrutiny, the story exposes itself as utter nonsense. It is the creation of fertile imaginations that have little choice but to speculate about the number after the Counter-Reformation stripped away the historic interpretation of prophecy. The story of the Beast of Belgium is apparently the brainchild of Joe Musser, a writer who invented the idea for a novel he wrote called *Behold the Pale Horse*.[1]

Others have pointed to bar codes, credit cards, and computer chip implants as the fulfillment of Revelation's 666 prophecy. But all are idle speculation. Others have applied the number to various prominent personages from Ronald Reagan to Pierre Elliott Trudeau—Reagan, as we noted earlier, because each of his three names has six letters (Ronald Wilson Reagan) and Trudeau because his license plate once included the number.

Mary Stewart Relfe has even tried to indict the Visa corporation as the beast, because she has managed to derive the number from the word "VISA." How did she do it?

"The folks at VISA took another beating from Relfe when she used strange logic to claim that it stands for the mark of the beast. She wrote, 'VISA is 666; Vi, *Roman* Numeral, is 6; the 'zz' sound, Zeta, the 6th character in the *Greek* alphabet, is 6; a, *English*, is 6 [implying that the letter a turned backwards is a 6]" (Mary Stewart Relfe, in W. M. Alnor, *Soothsayers of the Second Advent*, p. 85).

Such reasoning scarcely resembles the "wisdom" John talks about exercising in Revelation 13:18, but it demonstrates some of the lengths to which dispensationalists have been willing to go in order to accommodate their thinking to alternative interpretations of prophecy that reject the historicist approach and adopt a futurist one.

Others have come somewhat closer to the truth. Controversial Irish Protestant leader Ian Paisley is noted for identifying the Papacy as the beast of Revelation 13. Yet even he observed that the new European Parliament building, in which he holds a seat, has 679 seats. All of them have been allocated to various members of the Parliament except for one— seat number 666.[2]

Of course, such an arrangement could reflect the idea that nobody would want to insult someone by assigning them the seat, much the way that hotels never seem to have a thirteenth floor.

We must remember that merely having the number 666 on a document or seat is not enough to make someone antichrist. *All* of the identifying marks of Bible prophecy—enumerated in the previous chapter—must fit in order for a candidate to qualify. It is easy to make the number itself fit just about anything or anyone—but it is impossible to make all of prophecy's identifying marks apply with the kind of precision that they do the papal church-state.

Does the number fit the papal system to the letter as do the other identifying marks? Notice how the translators of *The New English Bible* have rendered Revelation 13:18: "Here is the key; and anyone who has intelligence may work out the number of the beast. The number represents a man's name, and the numerical value of its letters is six hundred and sixty-six."

Before the advent of Arabic numerals in the Western world (the numbering system we use today), letters of the alphabet received numerical values. This was true of Latin, Greek, and Hebrew. People in the ancient world commonly took the numerical equivalent of the letters of someone's name and added them up, giving the name a number.

Irenaeus, one of the Church Fathers of the second century, looked forward to the collapse of the Roman Empire, basing his expectation on Bible prophecy. He recognized that the fourth beast/kingdom of Daniel 7 would dissolve into 10 horns or divisions. Bible prophecy, he believed, predicted that the little horn power would then come out of the divided Roman Empire.

As to the mysterious number 666, Irenaeus pointed out that Christians would not be able to accurately discern its meaning until *after* the fall of the Roman Empire and the appearance of the little horn. "But, knowing the sure number declared by Scripture, that is, six hundred and sixty six, let them await, in the first place, the division of the kingdom into ten; then, in the next place, when these kings are reigning, and beginning to set their affairs in order, and advance their kingdom, [let them learn] to acknowledge that he who shall come claiming the kingdom for himself, and shall terrify those men of whom we have been speaking, having a name containing the aforesaid number, is truly the abomination of desolation" (*Against Heresies,* chap. 30, sec. 2).

Irenaeus nevertheless noticed that the Greek word *Lateinos,* a popular reference to the Latin kingdom, added up to 666. He found the title particularly interesting because of its clear connection with the fourth kingdom in Daniel 7.

In later years, after the establishment of the church-state papal system of Christian leadership, other scholars discovered that many references to papal Rome added up to 666, including titles found in three languages: Latin, Greek, and Hebrew. Repeated references to titles such as "Romiith" (Hebrew for "Roman kingdom") and "Italika Ekklesia" (Greek for "Italian church") have made their appearance in the writings of scholars all the way from Irenaeus's day to the present. Each of them adds up to 666 in their respective languages. It seems that there has never been a time in the history of Christianity when people have *not* noticed some connection between 666 and Rome.

Adam Clarke's famous Bible commentary, for example, points out: "We have already observed that the beast is the Latin kingdom or empire; therefore if this observation be correct, the Greek words signifying *the Latin kingdom* must have this number" (*Commentary on the New Testament,* comment on Revelation 13:18). Clarke then points out that the Greek term for the Latin kingdom—'*H Latine* Basileia—also adds up to 666 in the Greek language.

One of the things that Paul emphasized in describing the antichrist power was that it would involve somebody who proclaimed himself to be God: "Who opposeth and exalteth himself above all that is called God, or that is worshipped; so that he as God sitteth in the temple of God, shewing himself that he is God" (2 Thessalonians 2:4).

Daniel also emphasized that the little power would exalt itself to a position above God Himself: "And he shall speak great words against the most High, and shall wear out the saints of the most High, and think to change times and laws" (Daniel 7:25). "And it waxed great, even to the host of heaven; and it cast down some of the host and of the stars to the ground, and stamped upon them. Yea, he magnified himself even to the prince of the host, and by him the daily sacrifice was taken away, and the place of his sanctuary was cast down" (Daniel 8:10, 11).

The antichrist, according to the Bible, is an usurper. It claims to occupy the seat of God Himself. Writer Vittorio Messori interviews Pope John Paul II in the latter's best-selling book, *Crossing the Threshold of Hope*. The opening chapter of the book is John Paul II's answer to questions about the nature of the Papacy in the modern world.

Here's part of the question Messori put to the pope: "Confronted with the Pope, one must make a choice. The leader of the Catholic church is defined by the faith as the Vicar of Jesus Christ (and is accepted as such by believers). The Pope is considered the man on earth who represents the Son of God, who 'takes the place' of the Second Person of the omnipotent God of the Trinity" (p. 3).

Nowhere in the book does Pope John Paul II refute the notion that he "takes the place" of Jesus Christ. The Catholic Church has not changed its position on this idea since the Council of Trent. The essence of Messori's question to the pope is to determine how John Paul II personally feels about occupying the position of "Vicar of Christ," the one who stands in the place of Christ.

The pope readily admits that the designation contradicts the teaching of the gospel. "Returning to your question, I would like to recall the words of Christ together with my first words in St. Peter's Square: 'Be not afraid.' Have no fear when people call me the 'Vicar of Christ,' when they say to me, 'Holy Father,' or 'Your Holiness,' or use titles similar to these, which seem even inimical to the Gospel. Christ himself declared: 'Call no one on earth your father; you have but one Father in heaven. Do not be called "Master"; you have but one master, the Messiah' (Matthew 23:9, 10). These expressions, nevertheless, have evolved out of a long tradition, becoming part of common usage. One must not be afraid of these words either" (*ibid.,* p. 6).

John Paul II admits that no biblical basis exists for calling himself the Vicar of Christ or other such lofty titles. They come strictly from tradition and longtime usage. Not only does he establish himself (as have all popes through history) as standing in Christ's place; he includes, to some degree, the bishops under him.

Note his words: "The Pope is not the only one who holds this title. With regard to the Church entrusted to him, each bishop is *Vicarius Christi.* The Pope is Vicar of Christ with regard to the Church of Rome and, through that Church, of every Church in communion with it—a communion in faith as well as an institutional and canonical communion. Thus, if with this title one wants to refer to the dignity of the Bishop of Rome, one cannot consider it apart from the *dignity of the entire college of bishops,* with which it is tightly bound, as it is to the dignity of each bishop, each priest, and each of the baptized" (*ibid.,* p. 13).

Vatican Council II (1962-1965) made the following point: "For in virtue of his office, that is, as Vicar of Christ and pastor of the whole Church, the Roman Pontiff has full, supreme, and universal power over the Church. And he can always exercise this power freely" (Walter M. Abbott, S. J., ed., *The Documents of Vatican II,* p. 43).

In other words, the pope stands in for Christ as the head of the church on earth. Some might take that to mean that the pope assumes that he is head of merely the *Roman Catholic Church,* but that is not the case. He truly believes that he stands in for Christ as the head of *all* Christianity. In fact, according to a public declaration made by the Vatican in September of 2000 and ratified by the pope, churches that do not recognize the supremacy of the bishop of Rome are "deficient."

The document states that those churches not recognizing the episcopal form of church government and observing the Eucharistic rite are not to be true churches at all: "Therefore, since there exists a single Church of Christ, which subsists in the Catholic Church, governed by the Successor of Peter and by the Bishops in communion with him. The Churches which, while not existing in perfect communion with the Catholic Church, remain united to her by means of the closest bonds, that is, by apostolic succession and a valid Eucharist, are true particular churches. Therefore, the Church of Christ is present and operative also in these churches, even though they lack full communion with the Catholic Church, since they do not accept the Catholic doctrine of the Primacy, which, according to the will of God, the Bishop of Rome objectively has and exercises over the entire church.

"On the other hand, the ecclesial communities which have not preserved the valid Episcopate and the genuine and integral substance of the Eucharistic mystery, are not Churches in the proper sense" (Declaration *Dominus Iesus,* on the Unicity and Salvific Universality of the Jesus Christ and the Church [September 2000], sec. 17; this document came from the "Congregation for the Doctrine of the Faith," the new name for the office of the Inquisition).

Without question the pope still considers himself to be Vicarius Christ—the one who stands in the place of Christ. It is the term that probably best describes the Catholic understanding of the office of the Papacy, a concept has often been expressed through history in the Latin title for the Papacy: Vicarius Filii Dei—Vicar of the Son of God.[3]

Our Sunday Visitor is a long-running Catholic periodical still in print today. It has featured a Bureaus of Information column in which subscribers ask questions. The following question appeared in the April 18, 1915, edition: "What are the letters supposed to be in the Pope's crown, and what do they signify, if anything?" (Rev. John F. Noll, ed., *Our Sunday Visitor,* April 18, 1915, p. 3).

The answer is almost breathtaking: "The letters inscribed in the Pope's mitre are these: Vicarius Filii Dei, which is Latin for

Vicar of the Son of God. Catholics hold that the Church which is a visible society must have a visible head. . . . Hence to the Bishop of Rome, as head of the Church, was given the title 'Vicar of Christ'" *(ibid.)*.

In 1904 the office of the famous James Cardinal Gibbons of Baltimore, Maryland, answered a letter of inquiry about this papal title and stated that "the words are used by the Cardinal who imposes the tiara at the coronation of a Pope" (letter written by William F. Russell, secretary of James Cardinal Gibbons, in reply to H. J. Weaver, January 26, 1904; a facsimile can be viewed at *www.aloha.net/~mikesch/russell-letter.gif*).

Take this important title—Vicarius Filii Dei, which has embraced the office and function of the pope through the ages—and do a little bit of math. The operating language of the Roman church is Latin; until recently all masses were conducted in the language. If you add together the value of the Roman numerals in the title, the same way the ancients in John's day would have done it, you come to a rather startling conclusion. (Remember that in written Latin "U" and "V" were the same thing.[4]

V	5	**F**		**D**	500	
I	1	**I**	1	**E**		
C	100	**L**	50	**I**	1	
A		**I**	1			
R		**I**	1			
I	1					
U	5					
S						
	112	+	53	+	501	= **666**

If this was all the evidence we had, it might probably mean very little. With a little manipulation, you can make a lot of names add up to 666. What is striking about this title, however, is that not only do you not have to manipulate the name to make the math work, but also the title actually encapsulates the spirit of the papal church-state system and philosophy. That the numerical value of the letters adds up to 666 is simply the icing on the cake, so to speak, which supports the other identifying points given in the previous chapter.

Everything fits. No other power in human history matches the description given by Bible prophecy with such stunning accuracy. People have urged other candidates, but at best only one or two points correspond. Antichrist must be a perfect match for the Bible's description in order to qualify.

Ronald Reagan? Not likely. The endless string of candidates presented by modern dispensationalist thinkers does *not* fit with 100 percent accuracy. Their speculations don't even come close. Once Protestantism adopted the tenets of the Counter-Reformation early in the nineteenth century, Christians had little choice but to speculate idly about who or what the beast represents.

But Protestants did not always have such trouble.

---

[1] Evangelist David Wilkerson had the same novel turned into a movie. You'll find an exposé of the theory at a Web site developed to examine urban myths in Christianty at *www.truthorfiction.com/rumors/beastofbelgium.htm.*

[2] I must mention that Ian Paisley is *not* a futurist. He fully recognizes that the historic Christian position that antichrist comes out of a church-state union is fulfilled in the Papacy. I include this story simply to illustrate a growing sea of speculation about the number.

[3] You will find this title used in ancient Catholic documents such as the *Donation of Constantine.* The *Donation,* which supposedly made political concessions to the Papacy, was discovered in later years to be a deliberate forgery. Nonetheless, the Roman Christian leadership proclaimed the document as genuine for hundreds of years, and it used the papal title *Vicarius Filii Dei.*

[4] This is why to this day, on some older buildings, you will find the word "church" or "court" spelled "CHVRCH" or "COVRT."

Chapter 12

WHAT WE USED TO BELIEVE

Shawn Boonstra

I t was a terrible turn of events. Many people had anticipated that Lady Jane Grey, a Protestant, would take the throne of England after the death of Edward VI, but Mary beat her to it. And Mary was not kindly disposed toward Protestants. Before long, nearly 300 influential Protestants died lashed to a fiery stake, including many women and children. The ruthless slaughter earned the new queen the nickname "Bloody Mary."

On October 16, 1555, two men met and embraced in a little hollow outside Balliol College at Oxford. One of them was an elderly priest by the name of Hugh Latimer, the other a middle-aged former royal chaplain by the name of Nicholas Ridley. As Ridley held Latimer close, he said, "Be of good heart, brother, for God will either assuage the fury of the flame, or else strengthen us to abide it." Then the two of them knelt and shared a prayer together.

Having been stripped of his priestly office, Latimer was wearing a special shroud for the occasion. Ridley was wearing his trousers, but Latimer observed that pants might occasion more pain and advised him to give them to some poor man who could use them. Ridley stripped down to his shirt, and then stood on a stone and uttered, "O heavenly Father, I give unto thee most hearty thanks, for that thou hast called me to be a professor of Thee, even unto death: I beseech Thee, Lord God, take mercy upon this realm of England, and deliver the same from all her enemies."

Soldiers brought a chain and wrapped it around the bodies of the two men as they stood quietly on either side of the stake. When the smith started to nail the chain to the stake, Ridley grabbed it and said, "Good fellow, knock it in hard, for the flesh will have its course."

When they were secured, a man by the name of Shipside brought Ridley a bag of gunpowder to tie around his neck, which Ridley took to be a gift from God, since it would shorten his agony. "Do you have a bag for my friend Latimer?" he asked, worried that Latimer wouldn't have the same merciful end that he would. Someone brought another bag.

Everything was ready. After someone else lit the pile of wood they stood in and the flames began to lick up the sides of the stake, Hugh Latimer turned to his friend and spoke words that have echoed through the years: "Be of good comfort, Master Ridley; and play the man. We shall this day light such a candle, by God's grace, in England, as I trust shall never be put out."

In a few short moments the flames consumed Latimer. He was strangely calm throughout the entire incident, having always known it was coming. When the officer first came to arrest him after Mary had ascended the throne, Latimer said, "My friend, you are a welcome messenger."

Guards escorted him through Smithfield on the way to his trial. Many had been burned there alive for their faith. As he passed the site, he said, "Smithfield has long groaned for me."

As he waited in the Tower of London for his execution, he lost neither his Christian courage nor his sense of humor. One day, when it was particularly cold in the prison, he asked for a fire to keep warm. The prison keeper refused, until Latimer reminded him that if he were to die of exposure, it would cheat the authorities of the privilege of burning him at the stake.

When the time came to burn him alive, he no longer looked like a stooped-over old man of 83, but suddenly and proudly he stood perfectly upright, as if his fate were welcome. The fire didn't frighten him in the least. As the flames engulfed his body, he dipped his hands into them and brought them closer to his face. He was dead in mere moments, with onlookers convinced that he experienced little or no pain.

Ridley was not as fortunate. The fire was poorly built on his side of the stake, with the kindling on the bottom and the heaviest wood on top. The fire raged around his feet, but the heavy wood kept it from burning his vital organs. When he realized that only his legs were burning, he asked, in the name of Christ, that they mercifully let the fire burn the rest of him. His friend Shipside, who had provided the bag of gunpowder, heaped more wood on the fire, but that only made the problem worse. The fire simply refused to burn him except for his legs. His shirt was virtually untouched.

Horrified spectators watched him as he leaped up and down, writhing in agony and praying out loud that it would end. Finally one of the billmen reached into the flames with his weapon and pulled the heavy wood off the top. As soon as Ridley saw the flames leaping up, he wrenched his half-burned body to one side, where the flames lit the gunpowder around his neck.

It was finally over. But was it worth it? Why would two men be willing to die such a terrible death? Like many others, they could have avoided their awful fate by simply recanting what they had been teaching—but they would not.

Thomas Cranmer, on the other hand, *did* recant. After his appointment by Henry VIII as archbishop of Canterbury, he became one of the leading advocates of the Protestant Reformation. Naturally, when Mary came to the throne he was one of the first people she wanted eliminated. The authorities tried him along with Ridley and Latimer at Oxford and sentenced him to death.

After a number of years of cruel imprisonment, Cranmer received a written refutation of his Protestant teachings. The government promised him a life of comfort if he signed the document but the stake if he did not. His human nature trembled at the thought of death by fire, and he caved in and signed it.

The promise of release, however, was empty. In spite of his written retraction, Queen Mary still wanted him dead. On March 21, 1556, she ordered him to appear in front of a packed church at Oxford to recant his "heresies" publicly.

At Mary's request, a clergyman preached a special sermon prior to the execution. It depicted Cranmer as guilty of heinous crimes and admonished him to be penitent so that God would have mercy on his soul.

When the humiliating sermon concluded, the authorities asked Thomas Cranmer to give the congregation a public sign that he was indeed sorry for what he had taught. He was still wearing the dirty rags he had been given when stripped of his clerical office. Cranmer spoke from a special low stage, set up opposite the pulpit.

As he looked out over the congregation, he discovered new courage and made a tearful public confession of his sins—but not of the "sin" of teaching the Bible. Rather, he confessed the sin of having betrayed God. He had been miserable ever since he signed the recantation, he admitted.

Falling to his knees, he prayed out loud: "I have offended both against heaven and earth, more than my tongue can express. Where can I go? I am too ashamed to go to heaven, and I have no place to go here on earth! The only place I can run, Lord, is to You, and so I humble myself and say that though my sins are great, O Lord God, yet have mercy on me" (William Forbush, ed., *Foxe's Book of Martyrs,* p. 248).

Thus far it was exactly what the people expected to hear. When he finished praying, Cranmer received permission to speak a few words to the glory of God. For several minutes, he spoke on the fifth chapter of James, during which he warned against loving the world.

Then he said something that nearly brought the house down. "And now I come to the great thing which so much troubleth my conscience, more than any thing that ever I did or said in my whole life, and that is the setting abroad of a writing contrary to the truth, which now here I renounce and refuse, as things written with my hand contrary to the truth which I thought in my heart, and written for fear of death, and to save my life, if it might be; and that is, all such bills or papers which I have written or signed with my hand since my degradation, wherein I have written many things untrue. And forasmuch as my hand hath offended, writing contrary to my heart, therefor be punished; for when I come to the fire it shall first be burned.

"And as for the pope, I refuse him as Christ's enemy, and Antichrist, with all his false doctrines" *(ibid.)*.

Thomas Cranmer was true to his word. When they lit the fire beneath him, he stretched out the hand that had signed the recantation and held it unflinchingly in the flames.

Why would people such as Cranmer, Latimer, and Ridley rather face the cruelest of deaths than cooperate with the established church of the day? They clearly understood what Bible prophecy taught with regard to a coming apostasy in Christianity, and they were willing to take a stand against it. They knew of no "gap" in prophecy that covered up the Middle Ages.

Some modern Christians assume that the popular theories on prophecy today have always been around. Nothing could be further from the truth. Until the late nineteenth and early twentieth centuries most Christians saw a complete description of God's hand in history in Bible prophecy—including the time between the Crucifixion and now. It is only in relatively recent history—since about 1830—that Protestant Christians have adopted the position that the prophetic clock stopped at Calvary.

Latimer, Ridley, and Cranmer knew that the Bible doesn't ignore history between Christ's first and second advents. So did countless millions of others. Christians have traditionally held that the papal church–state system was the fulfillment of the predicted little-horn power.

When the soldiers set Latimer on fire, he prayed that his death would be a candle that would not soon be extinguished. Unfortunately, dispensationalism has nearly extinguished it. Modern Christians have virtually forgotten what the martyrs died for and at whose hand they died. Many circles now speak of the Protestant Reformation as a regrettable misunderstanding—even though not a single fundamental doctrine taught by the medieval church system has changed since the Council of Trent in the mid-1500s. The ideas that the Reformers challenged Rome still cherishes.

Yet, undeniably, something has changed. And if it's not Rome, it's Protestantism. The seed of futurism planted by Jesuit scholars Ribera and Bellarmine has finally taken root in Protestant thinking. The Counter-Reformation has been a smashing success. Such a success, in fact, that when the subject of the Papacy in Bible prophecy comes up, many Christians seem shocked, as if it were a completely new interpretation. But there is nothing new about it. It is as old as New Testament Christianity itself.

Popular modern thinking paints antichrist as a single individual who comes to power in the final few years of earth's history. However, the apostle Paul was clear that it was a power—and an influence—already taking shape in his day: "For the mystery of iniquity doth already work: only he who now letteth will let, until he be taken out of the way. And then shall that Wicked be revealed, whom the Lord shall consume with the spirit of his mouth, and shall destroy with the brightness of his coming" (2 Thessalonians 2:7, 8).

Paul is clear that the antichrist power was already beginning to take shape in his day and that it would blossom as soon as events removed the powers holding it in check. It would then continue to exist until Christ's coming destroyed it. The apostle's words completely exclude the possibility of a single individual being antichrist, because, as we have pointed out in a previous chapter, no single human being has lived from Paul's day until now.

The early church understood very clearly that antichrist would reach its fruition on the heels of the Roman Empire, not after a 2,000-year gap in prophetic time. The Church Father Jerome, for instance, stated: "[Paul] shows that that which re-strains is the Roman empire; for unless it shall have been de-stroyed, and taken out of the midst, according to the prophet Daniel, Antichrist will not come before that. If he had chosen to say this openly, he would have foolishly aroused a frenzy of persecution against the Christians; and then against the growing church" (in L. E. Froom, *Prophetic Faith,* vol. 1, p. 444).

When Jerome wrote this, the Roman Empire was still in power. It would not collapse until A.D. 476. He understood that Daniel had prophesied that the little-horn power would not bear sway over the earth until the 10 horns (political powers) replaced the fourth prophetic animal (the Roman Empire). As soon as Rome (the power that hindered the appearance of the antichrist) fell, Jerome explained, you could expect to see the antichrist power take over.

Jerome had no thought that antichrist would be a single individual at the end of history—someone removed from the rest of prophecy by a long period of time. Dispensationalists place the "secret" coming of Jesus before the appearance of such an antichrist, but Jerome taught differently. Not only did he understand that antichrist would naturally appear on the scene of world history once the Roman Empire collapsed, but he also understood it to be a power that would appear *within the church* and that would remain until the Second Coming.

Note Jerome's words: "And [Antichrist] may sit in the temple of God, either Jerusalem (as some think) or in the church (as we more truly think), showing himself as if he himself were Christ, and the Son of God. Unless, he says, the Roman empire has been previously desolated and Antichrist has preceded him, Christ will not come; who therefore will so come that he may destroy Antichrist" (in Froom).

The Church Father was not alone in this thinking. Before his time, Irenaeus, Tertullian, and other ancient Christian scholars also understood that the Roman Empire would eventually fracture into 10 segments, out of which antichrist would appear.

The list of those early Church Fathers who believed that antichrist would develop as a natural succession to the collapse of the Roman Empire and remain until the Second Coming is long. Of course, in the final analysis, it doesn't matter what the Church Fathers said. The Bible is our only infallible rule of faith and practice, yet the testimony of the ancient Christians clearly indicates that the prophetic charts of dispensationalists were completely unknown to them.

As time progressed, there came a growing awareness that Daniel's little horn and John's beast power bore a striking resemblance to the papal system. In fact, by the time the seventeenth century rolled around, Puritan evangelist Richard Baxter was able to say: "If the pope be not anti-Christ, he hath the ill-luck to appear so much like him."

The Synod of Rheims (A.D. 991) clearly demonstrates this awareness. Arnulf, the bishop of Rheims, had been accused of high treason against King Hugh Capet of France. Because of Arnulf's high position in the church, the king notified the pope of an impending trial, but received no reply. So he decided to try Arnulf without the pope's approval.

But church representatives claimed at the trial that because only the pope had the right to impeach bishops, it was outside of the king's jurisdiction to try Arnulf. The king didn't care. He removed the bishop of Rheims from office without Rome's permission.

The bishop of Orleans presented the main arguments in favor of the king's right to punish Arnulf, arguing eloquently from ancient documents that a local council was sufficient to try a bishop. Furthermore, he reasoned, the pope had no right to reverse the decisions of such ancient documents.

Then the bishop of Orleans uttered some surprisingly daring words: "What, in your eyes, reverend fathers, is that Pontiff, seated on a throne, and clad in purple and gold? If he hath not charity, and be puffed up with his learning only, he is Antichrist sitting in the temple of God, and demeaning himself as a god; he is like unto a statue in that temple, like a dumb idol, and to ask of him a reply is to appeal to a figure of stone." "There is, in the words of the apostle, division not only among the nations, but in the Churches, because the time of Anti-christ approaches; and, as the same apostle says, the mystery of iniquity is begun. It is manifest that in the decay of Roman power and the abasement of religion, the name of God is degraded with impunity by those who are perjured, and that the observance of His holy religion is despised by the sovereign pontiffs themselves" (in Froom, pp. 541, 542).

Even the Roman Catholic bishop of Orleans recognized in the Papacy an amazing similarity to the little horn. The words reached the ears of Pope John XV, who declared the decision of the trial null and void and then reinstated the bishop of Rheims.

The bishop of Orleans was by no means alone when he dared to label the papal church-state as antichrist. He was only one voice among a growing chorus of church leaders who identified the institution with the little horn of Daniel, the beast of Revelation, and what the apostle Paul called the "mystery of iniquity."

Perhaps one of the most notable voices to join the chorus in the early years of the Middle Ages was Joachim of Floris. Joachim understood the 1260 days of Bible prophecy to be a symbolic period of time representing 1260 literal years. In fact, he mistakenly assumed that the prophetic period would end around the year A.D. 1260, at which time he anticipated tumultuous events.

Although he loved the church, Joachim fearlessly attacked the institution of the Papacy as being one and the same as the "harlot" described in the book of Revelation. The final three plagues of Revelation, he said, would be especially directed at a corrupted church leadership, which he called the "new Babylon" (in Froom, p. 708).

Another cry against the papal antichrist system surfaced at the Synod of Regensberg (A.D. 1240 or 1241). The occasion for the synod was that Frederick II, ruler of the Holy Roman Empire, and Pope Gregory IX found themselves in a political dispute over supremacy in Europe. Medieval popes were quite open about their political aspirations and were not bashful in demanding their political "rights."

Eberhard II, the archbishop of Salzburg, came to the defense of the emperor by explaining that the little horn of Daniel 7 clearly identified the Papacy as antichrist. Unlike Jerome, who had to anticipate antichrist, Eberhard could look *back* over history and clearly see prophetic events fulfilled in the church.

The little horn, Eberhard said, is exactly fulfilled in the Papacy. It came out of a divided Roman Empire and uprooted three of the 10 divisions, just as Daniel foretold. Speaking of the pope, Eberhard declared: "Under the title of Pontifex Maximus, we discern, unless we are blind, a most savage wolf, with the garment of a shepherd; the Roman priests . . . have arms against all Christians; made great by daring, by deceiving, by bringing wars after wars, they slaughter the sheep, they cut them off, they drive away peace and harmony from the earth, they stir up internal wars, domestic insurrections from below, day by day they weaken more and more the energies of all, so that they revile the heads of all, they devour all, they reduce all to slavery." "Hildebrand, one hundred and seventy years before, first laid the foundations of the empire of Antichrist under the appearance of religion" (in Froom, p. 799).

Eberhard recognized that absolute power tends to corrupt those with authority, especially when those in power could blend religion and politics in such a way as to fortify their stranglehold. And he saw it happening during his own lifetime. His arguments focused on the fact that the Roman Empire had already collapsed. Therefore, he concluded, antichrist could be found by searching history after the collapse of the Western Roman Empire.

It never occurred to him to look for antichrist in the final seven years of earth's history, as dispensationalists do, because such an idea was unheard-of. Like all other Bible scholars of his day, he was of the historicist persuasion.*

He identified the Papacy as antichrist almost 300 years before the Protestant Reformation. Although a Catholic scholar who held an exceptionally high office in the church's hierarchy, he was honest enough with Scripture to admit the striking resemblance between the prophecies about antichrist and the papal institution.

When the Protestant Reformation took hold in Europe some centuries later, the historicist view of interpreting Bible prophecy continued to prevail. Wycliffe, Huss, Luther, Melancthon, Zwingli, Cranmer, Knox, and a host of other Reformers all identified the little-horn power with the Papacy. It is important to remember that most of the Reformers were Roman Catholics themselves. Many of them had no desire to leave their childhood church unless and until its behavior clearly identified it as antichrist.

When Martin Luther, a Roman Catholic monk of the Augustinian order, nailed his 95 theses to the door of the castle church in Wittenberg, they were a direct cry against the abuses of the papal system. He regarded them as propositions for debate, addressing subjects ranging from the papal sale of indulgences to the crucifixion of self and righteousness by faith. Luther did not intend to spread his theses among the common people. Rather, he was attempting to engage the church's scholarly community in a debate, one that would hold the Papacy responsible to Scripture.

But other people took the theses—originally written in Latin—and translated them into German for wide distribution. The invention of the printing press made it easy. Luther's propositions sparked a revolution in Germany, and when Albert of Mainz sent a copy to Rome, the pope caught wind of what was going on.

At first Pope Leo's reaction was surprisingly soft. He is reported to have made two comments: 1. "Luther is a drunken German. He will feel different when he is sober." 2. "Friar Martin is a brilliant chap. The whole row is due to the envy of the monks" (in Roland H. Bainton, *Here I Stand: A Life of Martin Luther,* p. 85).

In fact, Luther himself sent a personal message to Pope Leo, addressing him in affectionate terms and indicating that he, the pope, was of a character far superior to the moral quagmire that the papal system itself had fallen into. Luther insisted that he had no argument with Pope Leo but rather with a system that had become corrupt.

The pope's subdued response was short-lived, however. In time a papal bull, or official letter, condemned Luther's stand against the church and summoned him to a hearing. When the document reached Luther, he replied: "This bull condemns Christ himself. It summons me not to an audience but to a recantation. I am going to act on the assumption that it is spurious, though I think it is genuine. Would that Charles were a man and would fight for Christ against these Satans. But I am not afraid. God's will be done. I do not know what the prince should do unless to dissemble. I am sending you a copy of the bull that you may see the Roman monster. The faith and the Church are at stake. I rejoice to suffer in so noble a cause. I am not worthy of so holy a trial. I feel much freer now that I am certain the pope is Antichrist. . . . Farewell and pray for me" (in Bainton, p. 160).

Luther published a response entitled *Against the Execrable Bull of Antichrist* in which he stated that "whoever wrote this bull, he is Antichrist" (in Bainton, p. 161) and "I call upon you to renounce your diabolical blasphemy and audacious impiety, and, if you will not, we shall all hold your seat as possessed and oppressed by Satan, the damned seat of Antichrist, in the name of Jesus Christ, whom you persecute" (in Bainton, p. 163).

The war was on. The authorities seized Luther's books and publicly burned them. In retaliation Melancthon invited the faculty and students of the university to a book burning of their own. They committed papal constitutions, canon law, and works of Roman scholastic theology to the flames. Luther himself publicly burned the papal bull, later saying: "Since they have burned my books, I burn theirs. The canon law was included because it makes the pope a god on earth. So far I have merely fooled with this business of the pope. All my articles condemned by Antichrist are Christian. Seldom has the pope overcome anyone with Scripture and with reason" (in Bainton, p. 166).

We have no question about Luther's position on Bible prophecy. He regarded the papal church-state system as antichrist, and so did the other Reformers: John Wycliffe, John Huss, William Tyndale, John Calvin, Thomas Cranmer, Hugh Latimer, Nicholas Ridley, John Bradford, and John Foxe. All pronounced the Papacy "antichrist" because of what they had read in Scripture.

John Bunyan, the author of the greatly beloved *Pilgrim's Progress,* also believed that the Papacy was the little-horn power described in the book of Daniel. And *Pilgrim's Progress* has a number of thinly veiled allusions to that fact. He also published a lesser-known work entitled *The Ruin of Antichrist,* in which he exhorts Christian believers to be patient and wait for God, because the Lord Himself will destroy antichrist.

The translators of the King James Bible also saw the little-horn power in the institution of the Papacy. In the preface to their translation, addressed to James I and still printed in most King James Bibles, you'll find these words: "The zeal of Your Majesty toward the house of God doth not slack or go backward, but is more and more kindled, manifesting itself abroad in the farthest parts of *Christendom,* by writing in defence of the Truth, (which hath given such a blow unto that man of sin, as will not be healed)."

The impressive post-Reformation list of Christian leaders who understood Bible prophecy as historical and identified the Papacy as the beast power and little horn continues: Isaac Newton, Jonathan Edwards, George Whitefield, John Wesley, Charles Spurgeon, J. C. Ryle, and Martin Lloyd-Jones, among others.

Only since about 1830 have Protestants adopted the prophetic theories of the Jesuit Counter-Reformation. Rome has been more successful in undermining Scripture than it ever dreamed possible. By raising a dark dispensational curtain over the period between the crucifixion of Christ and the Second Coming, it has taken the spotlight off itself and shifted it to a nonexistent decoy—an obscure man at an obscure time in the obscure future.

Most of the Protestant world has bought it. Prophecy said it would happen.

---

* *Historicism,* you may recall, teaches that Bible prophecy has met its fulfillment in an unbroken chain throughout history. *Preterism,* on the other hand, claims that prophecy has all been fulfilled already, and *futurism* argues that most prophecy will be fulfilled in a short final burst at the end of time.

Chapter 13

THE DEADLY
WOUND WAS HEALED

Shawn Boonstra

On March 12, 2000, the pope did something that popes don't often do: he publicly apologized for sins committed by the Catholic Church during the past 2,000 years. In his "Day of Pardon" sermon he said: "We cannot fail to recognize *the infidelities to the Gospel committed by some of our brethren,* especially during the second millennium. Let us ask pardon for the divisions which have occurred among Christians, for the violence some have used in the service of the truth and for the distrustful and hostile attitudes sometimes taken towards the followers of other religions" ("Homily of the Holy Father, 'Day of Pardon,'" March 12, 2000, posted at the Vatican's Web site: *www.vatican.net*).

Alistair Cooke, the famous radio broadcaster, called the apology "the most significant event of recent times." He may be right. It *is* significant, because of what it represents—a new day for the Papacy. Rome may have met with a fatal blow in 1798 when one of Napoleon's generals pulled the pope off the throne, but it's not the end of the story.

According to Bible prophecy, Rome will reestablish what it has lost: "And I saw one of his heads as it were wounded to death; and his deadly wound was healed: and all the world wondered after the beast" (Revelation 13:3).

As we have noted in another chapter, the Papacy received its deadly wound in 1798. Many then assumed the institution was dead. The pope became a mere figurehead, a dim shadow of his past glory. According to the Bible, however, Rome would reverse its fortunes. The world would once again stand in amazement at the beast.

I'll be the first to admit that it's hard to believe. It seems impossible that the Vatican could ever be like it was, especially in light of Rome's apparently conciliatory nature. Things seem a far cry from the institution of some 500 years ago—or perhaps it only *appears* to be different.

If you dig a little deeper into John Paul II's apologies, you'll notice that he never really places the blame for what happened in medieval times on the papal institution itself. He speaks of truly regrettable things such as the crimes of "some of our brethren" and laments the "divisions . . . among Christians," but he never actually says, "I'm sorry the Papacy did these terrible things."

In fact, if you look at earlier apologies, you'll notice something significant. He's still trying to divert attention away from Rome. In a speech made on September 1, 1999, at the Vatican, John Paul II said that "the proximity of the Jubilee calls our attention to certain kinds of past and present sins that demand we invoke God's mercy in a special way. . . . I refer, above all, to the painful reality of the division among Christians. The wounds of the past, for which both sides share the guilt, continue to be a scandal for the world" ("Why Does the Church Ask Pardon for Past Sins?" news article, ZENIT, September 1, 1999).

Notice the pope's focus in this address. He is not apologizing for atrocities committed by the Inquisition or for the way church leadership relentlessly sought the lives of those who could not acknowledge the bishop of Rome as the supreme bishop. Instead he subtly shifts attention to the current division in Christianity, which is a genuine problem.

In focusing on the division within the Christian church rather than explicitly apologizing for the doctrines that led to crimes against humanity, the pope establishes himself as the leader of a conciliatory movement that seeks to reunite Christians under the banner of Rome.

People find themselves tempted to say, "The Papacy's not all that bad. Just look at the pope's apologies." But the papal system still believes what it established at the Council of Trent.

John Paul II doesn't *have* to apologize for the crimes of the Papacy because most of Protestant Christianity has long forgotten that it is the little-horn power depicted in Bible prophecy. The Counter-Reformation won, and it's time for the pope to reestablish himself as the undisputed head of Christianity now that the heat is off. The deadly wound has scabbed over. In fact, you can hardly tell where it was. The Reformation appears dead. We've virtually forgotten what we were fighting for.

Can you imagine what people such as Latimer and Ridley, who understood clearly what they were fighting, would say today? Probably they could have had a life of relative ease had they chosen to cooperate with the church leadership, but the Bible identified it as antichrist. And those stalwart believers chose the narrow road, standing on Scripture rather than on hundreds of years of ecclesiastical tradition. They lost their lives for it. Some estimates put the death toll in medieval times at approximately 50 million martyrs.

Life in Europe was no picnic for anybody who happened to disagree with the established church of the day. Standing for truth could cost everything. Then something important happened. The great hands of God's prophetic clock came to the appointed hour, and a door of mercy swung wide open through which people could escape persecution. "And the serpent cast out of his mouth water as a flood after the woman, that he might cause her to be carried away of the flood. And the earth helped the woman, and the earth opened her mouth, and swallowed up the flood which the dragon cast out of his mouth" (Revelation 12:15, 16).

The Bible consistently uses the symbol of a woman to portray God's people (see such passages as Jeremiah 6:2; 2 Corinthians 11:2; Ephesians 5:22-33). A pure woman, therefore, we would understand to represent a pure church, and conversely an impure woman would stand for an impure church (as in Hosea 2:5; 3:1; Ezekiel 16:15-58).

In Revelation 12 John sees a pure woman, representing

God's pure people. The woman faces persecution from the great red dragon, and God shelters her from its greatest attacks for "a time, and times, and half a time" (verse 14).[1] This period of time is equivalent to a year, two years, and half a year, or precisely 1,260 days—the same period of time that the Papacy would hold sway over the nations of the earth.

Eventually, in John's vision, the "earth" opens up to help the woman—and as the Middle Ages drew to a close, a new world emerged that promised freedom from religious persecution. Puritans, Baptists, and countless other tired, battered, and bruised Christians made their way to North America, seeking freedom.

To those who had never had a moment's peace, who had never been allowed to practice their Christian religion according to the dictates of their conscience, America was a golden door. It was the "earth" of Revelation 12, a place that ultimately became free from the persecuting marriage of church and state.

America's Constitution specifically states that the government "shall make no law respecting an establishment of religion, or prohibiting the free exercise thereof." It is a country where a clear wall of separation keeps the hands of the government off the church and the hands of the church off the government.

In America people can believe whatever their conscience tells them, even if they may be dead wrong. The United States is a nation in which people can coexist in spite of religious differences, and even defend each other's right to believe as they see fit. American liberty is the product of and reaction against centuries of church-state abuses. As a result, it was the place to which the persecuted masses of Europe fled.

The sad story portrayed in Bible prophecy, however, is that the earth makes another appearance in the next chapter of Revelation: "I beheld another beast coming up out of the earth; and he had two horns like a lamb, and he spake as a dragon" (Revelation 13:11).

John saw a second beast, but it emerged from the earth rather than the sea. In order to understand what the Bible is talking about, let's review what Scripture says about the first animal (political power) described in Revelation 13:1-8.

Verse 5 tells us that it would continue to exercise its power for 42 months, the same period of time as 1,260 days. (The calculation assumes an average month of 30 days.) The Papacy met its end in *exactly* 1,260 years. In 1798, exactly 1,260 years after the papal supremacy was established in A.D. 538, General Alexander Berthier—under orders from Napoleon—marched on Rome. Within 10 days Pope Pius VI found himself dethroned, imprisoned, and exiled. The French forces declared a new republic (Froom, *Prophetic Faith,* vol. 2, p. 755).[2]

G. Trevor wrote of this event: "The papacy was extinct: not a vestige of its existence remained; and among all the Roman Catholic powers not a finger was stirred" (*Rome From the Fall of the Western Empire,* p. 440, in Froom, vol. 3, p. 327).

It all happened precisely the *way* and exactly *when* the Bible said it would. The beast met with its deadly wound—but it was not a permanent injury. Today you can hardly notice the scar.

The Lateran Treaty of 1929 was a landmark in the restoration of the Papacy. Much had happened to humiliate Rome after 1798. By 1870, for example, the Italians had further diminished the Papacy by confiscating the lands it controlled in Italy, thereby uniting the nation of Italy under one political umbrella. Papal sovereignty found itself restricted to a few buildings, and the Italian government awarded an annual sum to the pope in exchange for the seizure.

The Holy See never recognized this arrangement, and popes considered themselves to be prisoners in the Vatican ("Lateran Treaty," *Columbia Encyclopedia,* 6th edition). The dispute over papal property became known as the "Roman Question." It was finally resolved on February 11, 1929, when Cardinal Gasparri, acting for Pope Pius XI, and Benito Mussolini, acting for King Victor Emmanuel III, signed a concordat that established Vatican City as a sovereign nation. Also, it authorized Roman Catholicism as the state religion of Italy (a provision that lasted until 1985). The Italian government considered—and considers—the person of the pope "sacred and inviolable" *(ibid.).* Primary and secondary schools in Italy must teach religion—another indication of the ongoing union of church and state.

It was a massive advancement for the Papacy. In fact, it was the first step down the path to total restoration. The wound was healing. The San Francisco *Chronicle,* in fact, titled its coverage of the event "Heal Wound of Many Years."[3]

Since that time the Papacy has constantly been on the ascendancy, gradually and patiently restoring through diplomacy what it lost after 1798. There's no question that the wound is healing, and the Bible says that Rome has a partner—the second beast.

This second beast has sometimes confused Bible scholars. In the past they have had little trouble understanding most of the symbols of Revelation that pointed to the papal church-state, such as "the beast," "Babylon," or "little horn." Enough history had transpired to permit clear identification.

The identity of the second beast, however, has not always been as clear. During the Middle Ages not enough history had passed to provide a precise identity. Besides, the second beast would not appear until after the first beast had received its deadly wound. (Revelation 13:12 describes the second beast as demanding worship for the first beast.) Today enough time has elapsed to permit understanding. The wound is healing, and there is little doubt as to the identity of the second beast.

Scripture provides several identifying points.

1. It is a "beast," which means that like other animals in Bible prophecy that we have studied, it is a political power—a government of some kind.

2. The first beast came up from the "sea," representing densely populated nations (see Revelation 17:15), whereas the second animal comes up from just the opposite—the "earth." It is a nation that does *not* come up in the Mediterranean world, but elsewhere.

3. The "earth" was the place that opened up to help the persecuted masses of Europe in Revelation 12. This second power appears in the place to where the persecuted flee.

4. The second political power appears at the time when the first receives its deadly wound, since Revelation 13:12 says that the second beast is instrumental in securing the adoration of the world for the beast after its wound has healed. The first beast received its wound, as we have pointed out, in 1798.

5. The second beast *looks* like a lamb, but speaks like a dragon. All through the Bible, lambs clearly symbolize Christ. In fact, the book of Revelation uses this symbol for Christ no fewer than 28 times. It is a power that appears to be Christlike, but when it eventually opens its mouth it reveals its true nature—that of the dragon.

6. The first beast had crowns on its horns, because the divisions of the Western Roman Empire were *kingdoms*. We find no crowns mentioned in connection with the second beast's head, because this power is *not* a kingdom.

We can have little doubt about which earthly power the second beast represents. No other nation in the history of Planet Earth fits the description as neatly as does the United States of America. Take another look.

1. America is a political entity.

2. America developed in a relatively sparsely populated area.

3. America was a refuge for the persecuted masses of Europe and is still understood to be a refuge for the underprivileged and persecuted of the whole world.

4. America was founded as a nation in 1776, after the close of the Middle Ages. Ironically, the power and influence that America currently enjoys was especially the result of developments following World War I, in the early 1900s—about the same time that the papal wound started healing.

5. America claims to be built on Christian principles: "One nation, under God, indivisible." The world perceives it to be a Christian nation. Yet, according to Bible prophecy, the United States will one day speak as a dragon.

6. America has a representative form of democracy, sometimes called a republic—perhaps the most successful republic in human history. It is not a kingdom.

According to Bible prophecy, even though it seems lamblike enough, America will build a bridge to Rome that will restore the Papacy to its former glory. The United States, according to this prophecy, will start to speak like a dragon—in other words, it will echo the power that influenced the papal system.

Impossible? Not at all.

At its founding America deliberately organized in opposition to European models of government. The Founders remembered the oppression caused by the marriage of church and state in medieval Europe, and they refused to permit a union of church and state—which historically has proven itself vulnerable to corruption of power—to gain a foothold in the New World. The new nation established a clear wall of separation to keep the hands of the church off the civil government and the hands of the civil government off the church.

Thomas Jefferson wrote that America was a place where every person has the right to choose their own religion without incurring discrimination. "No religious test shall ever be required as a qualification to any office or public trust under the United States" (Constitution of the United States, Article VI).

He also said that "it is error alone which needs the support of government. Truth can stand by itself" (*Notes on the State of Virginia*, 1781-1785, in Saul K. Padover, *The Complete Jefferson*, p. 675).

Jefferson was right. Truth *will* stand on its own. God never intended for the government to legislate love for Him. Coerced obedience is not real love. People widely recognized in Jefferson's day that the marriage of temporal and spiritual authority had corrupted and crippled medieval Europe, and so they determined that America would be a place free from that kind of persecution.

"Is uniformity attainable? Millions of innocent men, women, and children, since the introduction of Christianity, have been burnt, tortured, fined, imprisoned; yet we have not advanced one inch towards uniformity. What has been the effect of coercion? To make one half the world fools and the other half hypocrites. To support roguery and error all over the earth" (in Padover, p. 676).

"Let us reflect that having banished from our land that religious intolerance under which mankind so long bled and suffered, we have yet gained little if we countenance a political intolerance as despotic, as wicked, and capable of as bitter and bloody persecutions. . . . Error of opinion may be tolerated where reason is left free to combat it. . . . It is proper that you should understand what I deem the essential principles of our government. . . . Equal and exact justice to all men, of whatever state or persuasion, religious or political; . . . freedom of religion; freedom of the press; freedom of person under the protection of the *habeas corpus;* and trial by juries impartially selected" (Thomas Jefferson, "First Inaugural Address," March 4, 1801, in Padover, pp. 385, 386).

As a result of such thinking, the First Amendment to the U.S. Constitution states: "Congress shall make no law respecting an establishment of religion, or prohibiting the free exercise thereof; or abridging the freedom of speech, or of the press; or the right of the people peaceably to assemble, and to petition the Government for a redress of grievances."

In other words, Americans are perfectly free to believe as they see fit. They have complete freedom *of* religion and even perfect freedom *from* religion, if they so choose.

The absolute separation of church and state was the lamblike platform on which the United States was built. Freedom of thought is a lamblike quality. God did not force Adam and Eve to obey against their will. Jesus will not force people into the kingdom of heaven against their will. Neither should Christians force people into church pews or to adhere to a certain creed against their will.

America used to echo this sentiment. In recent history, however, we have seen a dramatic shift in the tenor of American religious thought. Some prominent and influential Christians are no longer content with the wall of separation. In fact, some of them have begun to deny that it ever existed at all. The reason? America has become morally corrupt, and the only solution (according to some) is for Christians to seize the reins of government and *legislate* morality.

Listen to some of the things prominent Christian leaders have been saying lately.[4]

"If Thomas Jefferson were alive today, I believe he would not only lead the struggle to scale the 'wall of separation' between church and state, but that he would also provide the ladders" (Richard McMunn, editor of *Columbia* magazine, a publication of the Knights of Columbus, February 1989).

"The time has come to restore the vital relationship between the church and state, between religion and law. . . . If church and state journeying together are to engage in friendly conversation, there cannot be a towering, impregnable wall between them" (Cardinal Anthony J. Bevilacqua, archbishop of Philadelphia, Oct. 1, 1989).

Some readers might argue that we might well expect sentiments such as these from leading Roman Catholic thinkers, who are merely repeating the opinions that the Papacy has held for hundreds of years. The startling thing, however, is the number of *Protestant* leaders who have started talking about uniting church and state.

"I believe this notion of the separation of church and state was the figment of some infidel's imagination" (W. A. Criswell, former president of the Southern Baptists, in a CBS television interview, Sept. 6, 1984).

"I want you to just let a wave of intolerance wash over you. I want you to let a wave of hatred wash over you. Yes, hate is good. . . . Our goal is a Christian nation. We have a biblical duty, we are called on by God to conquer this country. We don't want equal time. We don't want pluralism" (Randall Terry, Operation Rescue, in *The News Sentinel,* Aug. 8, 1993).

"Nobody has the right to worship on this planet any other God than Jehovah. And therefore the state does not have the responsibility to defend anybody's pseudo-right to worship an idol" (Joseph Morecraft, Chalcedon Presbyterian Church, speaking at the Biblical Worldview and Christian Education Conference, Aug. 8, 1993).

"I believe that the Christian Coalition will be the most powerful political force in America by the end of the decade" (Pat Robertson, *America at the Crossroads* video, 1990).

The list of quotations could go on for pages. Let's be honest, though. Does this sound more like a lamb or a dragon? Without question, the tenor of religious thought in America has decidedly swung in favor of uniting church and state.

We need to be clear that the issue is not whether or not these are sincere Christians speaking. Most or perhaps all of them are. The real issue is whether or not God is in the business of forcing people into the kingdom and whether or not the Papacy has succeeded in making us forget the past. Protestants are eagerly bridging the gulf back to the papal church-state system.

In fact, many Protestants have completely forgotten what Protestantism is all about. They have little comprehension of the issues of the Reformation, which some now think were little more than a regrettable misunderstanding.

Listen to what some Protestants now say. (I refer the reader again to footnote 4.)

"I don't know anyone more dedicated to the great fundamental doctrines of Christinity than the Catholics" (W. A. Criswell).

"I've found that my beliefs are essentially the same as those of orthodox Roman Catholics" (Billy Graham).

"I'm eradicating the word Protestant even out of my vocabulary. . . . I'm not protesting anything. . . . It's time for Catholics and non-Catholics to come together as one in the Spirit and one in the Lord" (Paul Crouch, Trinity Broadcasting Network).

"It's time for Protestants to go to the shepherd [the pope] and say, 'What do we have to do to come home?'" (Robert Schuller).

"We have differences, but on the ancient creeds and the core beliefs of Christianity we stand together" (Charles Colson).

Obviously the Bible speaks of Christian unity. God never intended for His church to fragment into literally hundreds or thousands of denominations that scrap with each other. The biblical concept of Christian unity, however, does not rest on compromise, but on truth.

A deliberate and stealthy attempt to reestablish the Papacy has hidden under the banner of unity, and it has been tremendously successful. Most of the Christian world looks upon the Papacy as, at best, a positive thing, and, at worst, benign. Hence the papal "apologies." The voices of opposition are few and far between.

Rome has been patient. The Counter-Reformation has finally paid off. Those in favor of tearing down the wall of separation are most often of a futurist mind-set. The futurism invented by the Counter-Reformation and later adopted into Protestantism during the nineteenth and twentieth centuries has wiped out most Protestants' memories. The Papacy is nearly free again to do as it pleases.

American Christian leaders now herald the pope as a

Christian "evangelist," and have sought cooperation and even reunion with Rome. Many point to the secular culture of America as something that Catholics and Protestants can conquer together. Consider the words of Charles Colson: "This is the chasm—the culture war—in the face of which evangelicals and Catholics find themselves to be allies. This is the context in which we can learn a great deal about and from each other. And we can learn from our differences as well as from our similarities" (*Evangelicals and Catholics Together: Toward a Common Mission,* p. 31).[5]

It's a new day for Rome. The pope travels the world as a political hero.[6] The wound has been healed. In fact, you can scarcely see the scar.

---

[1] A "time" is the equivalent of a "year." Daniel 4:25, for example, tells us that Nebuchadnezzar lost his sanity for seven "times," or years.

[2] It's interesting to note that it was the Franks, or the French, who were the first European tribe to grant the Papacy control over Europe when Clovis, king of the Franks, declared his allegiance to the bishop of Rome in A.D. 508. Thus the same "horn" that enthroned the Papacy eventually dethroned it.

[3] The San Francisco *Chronicle* was referring, of course, to the "Roman Question"—the secondary wound that Italy had inflicted on the Vatican in 1870. The uncanny reference to Revelation 13, I believe, was made unwittingly, but it is still of significance for students of Bible prophecy.

[4] These quotations in no way are an attempt to belittle or dismiss the Christian experience of those quoted. I do not wish to indict individuals. Many of them are fine Christian leaders who have led many souls to Christ. But I believe that many of them are unwittingly echoing the sentiments of the papal system. I furnish the quotations as evidence of the current religious atmosphere of America.

[5] A stunning document entitled *Evangelicals and Catholics Together: Toward a Common Mission* was released in 1994. This collaborative effort of some leading Catholic and evangelical scholars in America emphasized the importance of uniting on common causes and forgetting the past.

[6] Some have attributed the collapse of Communism in large part to the efforts of the pope. *Time* magazine in 1984 released an issue describing the Polish Solidarity movement and the collapse of Communism as a cooperative effort between President Ronald Reagan and John Paul II. Once Communism stood in the way of worldwide papal influence—now it no longer does. A popularized book on John Paul II's political aspirations is Malachi Martin's *The Keys of This Blood.*

Chapter 14

THE KING IS COMING

Shawn Boonstra

S ome years ago a great Protestant convention met in a city of the Midwest. Delegates and preachers assembled from all over the world. At one of the meetings a young preacher received an invitation to speak on the second coming of Christ. He opened his remarks by saying, "I don't believe in a literal, personal return of Jesus. I believe that His coming will be seen in better politics, better peace plans among nations, church union, and the spirit of understanding among men."

Then turning to one of the ministers seated behind him on the rostrum, he asked, "Don't you think so, Dr. Brown?"

The old man of God quietly arose from his seat and stood beside his younger fellow minister, and repeated in a voice full of emotion, " 'This same Jesus, which is taken up from you into heaven, shall so come in like manner as ye have seen him go into heaven' [Acts 1:11]." Then he quietly sat down.

The Bible is full of references concerning the Second Coming.

"And Enoch also, the seventh from Adam, prophesied of these, saying, Behold, the Lord cometh with ten thousands of his saints" (Jude 14).

Job, in the hour of his grief, said: "For I know that my re-deemer liveth, and that he shall stand at the latter day upon the earth" (Job 19:25).

The psalmist said: "Our God shall come, and shall not keep silence" (Psalm 50:3).

The prophet Zephaniah said: "The great day of the Lord is near, it is near, and hasteth greatly, even the voice of the day of the Lord: the mighty man shall cry there bitterly. That day is a day of wrath, a day of trouble and distress, a day of wasteness and desolation, a day of darkness and gloominess, a day of clouds and thick darkness" (Zephaniah 1:14, 15).

Anyone who reads and believes the New Testament cannot have any shadow of a doubt about Christ's promise that He is coming back again to this world. He spoke of it often and in plain language.

The Gospel of John quotes Him as having said: "Let not your heart be troubled: ye believe in God, believe also in me. In my Father's house are many mansions: if it were not so, I would have told you. I go to prepare a place for you. And if I go and prepare a place for you, I will come again, and receive you unto myself; that where I am, there ye may be also" (John 14:1-3).

Nothing could be less ambiguous than His words. The historical record in the four Gospels and the teachings in the Epistles are certainly clear. The gist of the reports is: "He was here once, and while He was here He predicted His sure return. The Son of God, He never lied. In fact, He not only told the truth, He *is* 'the Truth.'"

In a certain court case, a lawyer told the judge that his client couldn't be present in the courtroom. The judge became very angry and irritated that the person was absent. "Can you give me three good reasons this person is not here?" he growled at the lawyer.

"Yes," said the attorney, "I can. In the first place he died this morning. In the second place—"

"Stop," the judge shouted. "You don't need any more reasons. Your first one is sufficient."

Now, if Jesus mentioned only once and the apostles mentioned only once that He would return to earth again, even that would be reason enough for us to believe Him. But they promised and spoke of the Second Coming many times.

Paul calls it a "glorious appearing" (Titus 2:13). Peter preached about the time when God would send Jesus (Acts 3:20). Elsewhere he wrote: "And when the chief Shepherd shall appear, ye shall receive a crown of glory that fadeth not away" (1 Peter 5:4).

John, the beloved disciple, ends the book of Revelation with a promise and a prayer. First of all we have the promise of the Savior: "Surely I come quickly," followed then by John's prayer: "Even so, come, Lord Jesus" (Revelation 22:20).

James, Jesus' own brother, also believed that Jesus would return: "Be patient therefore, brethren, unto the coming of the Lord" (James 5:7). And he added: "The coming of the Lord draweth nigh" (verse 8).

Is it not strange that Bible-believing Christians accept a secret rapture teaching without the Bible having a single reference to it? Notice the order of events as taught by the dispensationalist.

1. Rapture (resurrection of righteous, saints being caught up to heaven).

2. Tribulation.

3. Second Coming in glory and power.

4. Millennium.

Now compare this with the order of events given in the Bible.

MATTHEW 14

1. Tribulation (verse 29).
2. Darkening of sun and moon, falling of stars (verse 29).
3. Second Coming in power and glory (verse 30).
4. Saints caught up to heaven (verse 31).

MARK 13

1. Tribulation (verse 24).
2. Darkening of sun and moon, falling of stars (verses 24, 25).
3. Second Coming in power and glory (verse 26).
4. Saints caught up to heaven (verse 27).

LUKE 21

1. Tribulation events (verses 25, 26).

2. Signs in the sun, moon, and stars (verse 25).

3. Second Coming in power and glory (verse 27).

1 Thessalonians 4

1. Second Coming in power and glory (verse 16).

2. Resurrection of righteous (verse 16).

3. Saints caught up to heaven (verse 17).

Revelation 6

1. Earthquake, darkening of sun, moon turned to blood, falling of stars (verses 12, 13).

2. Second coming of Jesus in power and glory (verses 14-17).

Joel 2

1. Darkening of sun and moon (verse 31).

2. Second Coming in power and glory (verse 32).

Although the Bible spells out the order of events a number of times, never once do we find the order proposed by dispensationalists. Because they are told that the majority of the Bible is not meant for Christians and that most of the book of Revelation talks of a tribulation that Christians will have no part in, believers in the secret rapture feel no need to concern themselves with the details of the events. They forget that the very purpose of the book of Revelation is to "shew unto *his servants* things which must shortly come to pass" (Revelation 1:1).

In previous chapters we saw how the 1,260-year time of tribulation was fulfilled, beginning in A.D. 538, when Justinian's decree gave the bishop of Rome, Pope Vigilius, full power, and ended in the year 1798, when General Berthier arrested the pope.

It would seem natural, then, for students of the Bible to look in Joel 2, Matthew 24, Mark 21, Luke 13, and Revelation 6 for the events that follow the tribulation and precede the Second Coming. Somewhere in the eighteenth and nineteenth centuries we would expect an earthquake, a dark day, the moon looking like blood, and the stars falling from the heavens. The next event we should look forward to is not a rapture but the heavens departing as a scroll as Christ returns in power and glory.

A Great Earthquake—At the exact moment on God's time clock, it happened. November 1, 1775, All Saints' Day in Lisbon, Portugal, at 9:30 a.m. the ground began to tremble, tearing fearsome fissures in the walls of public edifices. Homes, churches, government buildings, and palaces swayed like reeds in the wind for two minutes that seemed like eternity. Masonry crumbled, marble beams and pillars tore like tissue, and roofs and walls crashed to the ground.

Not just Lisbon felt the effects. The quake leveled the North African city of Fes, 400 miles away, and its sister city, Meknes, causing heavy loss of life. It shook other European cities as well, including Strasbourg—1,100 miles distant. The tectonic activity disturbed rivers and lakes as far away as Scandinavia, and a tidal wave struck the island of Barbados in the Caribbean, some 4,000 miles away (C. M. Maxwell, *God Cares*, vol. 2, pp. 194, 195).

Historian Ernest Montieth visited the Gosling Memorial Library in St. Johns, Newfoundland, where he found a book that indicates that people noticed the effects of the earthquake even in that Canadian province. "I have been informed by several respectable individuals," the author wrote, "that at the time of the great earthquake at Lisbon, in 1755, the effects were felt at Bonavista. The sea retired, and left the bed of the harbour dry for the space of ten minutes, when it again flowed in and rose to an unusual height, overflowing several meadows for about the same space of time as it had retired, and the waters on each side of the cape were greatly agitated" (J. Ernest Montieth, *The Lord Is My Shepherd*, p. 3).

The Sun Black as Sackcloth of Hair—The prophecy says that after the earthquake there would be a dark day. The earth, of course, has had many gloomy overcast days in its history, but the black Friday of May 18, 1780, stands above them all. The darkness started in Connecticut at about 10:00 a.m., coming from the southwest. From there it moved rapidly northward over several states. Dogs, chickens, and birds realized that something was unusual. By noon many people were thoroughly frightened, thinking the day of doom had certainly arrived.

One of the great American poet John Greenleaf Whittier's

lesser-known poems is one called "Abraham Davenport." It vividly portrays a scene that took place in the governor's council during the Dark Day of 1780. The Dark Day caused such an impression that the legislature adjourned. Colonel Davenport dared to propose a different course. Here is how the poem describes what happened.

> "He rose, slowly cleaving with his steady voice
> The intolerable hush. 'This well may be
> The Day of Judgment which the world awaits;
> Be it so or not, I only know
> My present duty, and my Lord's command
> To occupy till He come. So at the post
> Where He hath set me in His providence,
> I choose, for one, to meet Him face to face,
> No faithless servant frightened from my task,
> But ready when the Lord of Harvest calls;
> And therefore, with all reverence, I would say,
> 'Let God do His work, we will see to ours.
> Bring in the candles.' And they brought them in."

Sir William Herschel, the great astronomer of the late eighteenth and early nineteenth centuries, reportedly said that the Dark Day in North America was one of those phenomena that will always be read of with interest but which philosophy will be at a loss to explain.

The Moon Became Blood—The next item in prophecy is the moon turning to blood. The evening of the Dark Day, the people looked up at the night sky to see the moon blood-red in color. Afterward, a writer in New York commented: "It seems to me that the next sign should be the falling of the stars. We have seen the Dark Day, and though I didn't see it, I was informed that the moon looked like blood the following night."

The Stars of Heaven Fell Unto the Earth—He was absolutely right. The next sign was the falling of the stars. W. G. Fisher, astronomer from Howard University, said: "On the morning of the 13th of November, 1833, the people of the United States were awakened to see the stars falling."

A French astronomer, Camille Flammarion, compared the falling stars to the density of a snowstorm. Peter McMillan, in the magazine *The Telescope,* estimated that from 100,000 to 200,000 stars fell per hour.

The amazing event had begun to attract attention along the Eastern seaboard by about 9:00 the previous evening. By 2:00 in the morning the display was bright enough to awaken people. On the Great Plains, American Indians recorded the events on their calendars and named the ensuing season as the "Plenty Stars" or "Storm of Stars" winter.

In Manitoba, Canada, a visitor to the Assiniboine tribe met an old Indian who had a stick with a notch on it for every year of his life. He was then 104 years old, and recalled that he remembered from his childhood the time when the great white God of heaven became angry and spat fire out of His mouth. Then he pointed out the notch, indicating the year of this occurrence. The year was 1833 (Montieth, p. 5).

A Canadian newspaper explained the event as an "atmospheric phenomenon," describing "the most splendid exhibition of meteoric lights perhaps ever seen." "Those who witnessed the scene were variously affected, some with agreeable delight, others with apprehensions of evil, but all with astonishment. Some gave character to their feelings by exclaiming, 'The sky was falling to pieces'" (*ibid.,* p. 4).

As historian C. Mervin Maxwell points out, these events were important in three respects:

1. *Their magnitude.* All of them attracted worldwide attention and made an impact on the people of their time.

2. *Their location.* They occurred in Europe and North America, where people were studying the Bible and pondering the prophecies and would be ready to perceive their importance. A dark day over the Sahara or in New Guinea would have said little about the coming of Christ to cannibal headhunters or Muslim nomads.

3. *Their timing.* They took place at the exact time and in the right order (*God Cares,* vol. 2, pp. 201, 202).

We are living between verses 13 and 14 of Revelation 6. The events of verse 13 have already taken place while those of verse 14 are yet to come. Soon the heavens will depart as a scroll, and every mountain and island will be removed. From the majestic Canadian Rockies to the Andes of South America, from the Swiss Alps to the Himalayas, from Bermuda to the British Isles and to the Hawaiian Islands, the event will affect every corner of the globe, for God has His faithful people scattered through every "nation, and kindred, and tongue, and people" (Revelation 14:6).

Yes, Jesus is coming back to our world in power and great glory, as King of kings and Lord of lords, and "every eye shall see Him" (Revelation 1:7). He didn't give up on this prodigal planet. Remember, He left His blood here, and His promise to return is sure. He's coming back for you so that you can live with Him forever, if you so choose (see John 14:1-3).

And there will be no dreadful, bloody future after His return, with seven years of tribulation followed by 1,000 years of sin and death and bloody sacrifices and wars, as taught by the dispensational idea of the future. Scripture simply does not know of such a scenario, even though novels and Hollywood movies do.

Jesus is coming to end forever the sin and suffering that has so long plagued our planet and its people. Can you imagine an unceasing life with Jesus in a new world of restored Edenic beauty, with no sickness and sorrow, no disaster and death? The Savior calls you to prepare now for this soon-coming day, as He entreats: "Be ye also ready: for in such an hour as ye think not the Son of man cometh" (Matthew 24:44).

Chapter 15

THE BLESSED HOPE

Shawn Boonstra

The Second Coming is perhaps the most talked-about subject in the Bible. Some scholars have estimated that for every time the Bible mentions Jesus' first advent, it refers to the Second Coming eight times. As many as one out of 11 verses in the New Testament speak of it.

With that much coverage, you'd think that Christians would universally agree about the manner of Christ's return. The trouble is that many people approach the doctrine of the Second Coming much the way they would a salad bar: choosing what they like and leaving the rest behind. When a Bible text appears to support their theory, they heartily adopt it. But when it doesn't fit, they quietly ignore it.

There doesn't need to be any confusion. The weight of biblical evidence presents a rather clear pattern of events associated with the Second Advent. Even a cursory examination of the subject firmly establishes a number of things that we can know for certain.

Jesus Will Literally and Physically Return—Some people seem to have given up on the idea that Jesus will really return. They treat the Second Coming not as a literal event but rather as a metaphor for some sort of "spiritual awakening" in an individual's life. Some have even said that the Second Coming merely symbolizes becoming a Christian: Jesus figuratively returns when a person accepts His teachings.

Jesus Himself, however, recognized a literal Second Coming. "Let not your heart be troubled: ye believe in God, believe also in me. In my Father's house are many mansions: if it were not so, I would have told you. I go to prepare a place for you. And if I go and prepare a place for you, *I will come again,* and receive you unto myself; that where I am, there ye may be also" (John 14:1-3).

"I will come again." No ifs here, or any indication that it may be conditional. In fact, Jesus used the present tense to emphasize the certainty of it—literally: "I am coming again." We find not even a hint that Jesus was speaking metaphorically. Reading this passage, one can reach only one of three conclusions: (1) Jesus didn't know what He was talking about; (2) Jesus was willfully deceiving the disciples; or (3) Jesus was telling the truth. Christians find themselves left with only one option: Jesus was telling the truth. He *will* come again.

Yet the manner of His return remains an area of dispute among Christians. Exactly *how* will Jesus arrive? Perhaps a better way to put it would be: Exactly *who* will return? I have heard some people—for instance, Jehovah's Witnesses—claim that Jesus will appear as an ethereal spirit being. What does the Bible say?

Let's go back to where we began this book. The disciples spent the Crucifixion weekend hiding because they feared that they might be the next ones to hang on a cross. Then stories started coming back to them from people who claimed to have seen Jesus alive. Was it possible?

Pay attention carefully to what the Bible says happened next. "And as they thus spake, Jesus himself stood in the midst of them, and saith unto them, Peace be unto you. But they were terrified and affrighted, and supposed that they had seen a spirit. And he said unto them, Why are ye troubled? and why do thoughts arise in your hearts? Behold my hands and my feet, that it is I myself: handle me, and see; for a spirit hath not flesh and bones, as ye see me have. And when he had thus spoken, he shewed them his hands and his feet. And while they yet believed not for joy, and wondered, he said unto them, Have ye here any meat? And they gave him a piece of a broiled fish, and of an honeycomb. And he took it, and did eat before them" (Luke 24:36-43).

Jesus went to great lengths to prove that He had literally and physically risen from the dead. It was not a spook that appeared in the room with the disciples, but rather Jesus in the flesh. To drive the point home, Jesus asked the disciples to touch Him, and then He ate something in front of them.

Christ rose from the dead literally, with a physical body. What does that have to do with the Second Coming? Everything. Notice what happened a few weeks later when Jesus went to heaven. "And when he had spoken these things, while they beheld, he was taken up; and a cloud received him out of their sight. And while they looked stedfastly toward heaven as he went up, behold, two men stood by them in white apparel; which also said, Ye men of Galilee, why stand ye gazing up into heaven? this same Jesus, which is taken up from you into heaven, shall so come in like manner as ye have seen him go into heaven" (Acts 1:9-11).

The angels told the disciples that "this Jesus" (the original Greek has no word for "same")—the One who had just ascended—this Jesus is coming back the same way He went. The Jesus who went to heaven had a physical body and literally went to heaven. This Jesus—the One with a physical body—will return.

The passage in Acts also introduces the next thing of which we can be absolutely certain. Notice some of the verbs used to describe what the disciples were doing: "beheld," "looked," "gazing," "seen." They are significant. The disciples *watched* Jesus go, and the angel told them that Jesus would return in the "same manner." The arrival of Jesus will be *visible*.

Every Eye Will See Him—Jehovah's Witnesses are fond of telling people that Jesus secretly returned to earth to set up His kingdom in 1914. Notice, for example: "Christ Jesus comes, not again as a human, but as a glorious spirit person. . . . Since no earthly men have ever seen or can see the Father, they will be unable to see the glorified Son" (*Let God Be True,* pp. 196, 197).

Jehovah's Witnesses are not alone when it comes to teaching an "invisible" or "secret" return of Christ. Proponents of the secret rapture theory also advocate that when Christ comes

He will secretly steal away the saints. Notice, however, what the Bible says on the subject: "Behold, he cometh with clouds; and *every eye shall see him,* and they also which pierced him: and all kindreds of the earth shall wail because of him. Even so, Amen" (Revelation 1:7).

John tells us that *every* eye will observe Christ when He returns, and this includes the wicked, who will wail when He appears. The secret rapture theory claims that only the saved will see Jesus when He returns—an idea clearly out of harmony with what the authors of the Bible believed.

Today the world witnesses big events through the miracle of electronic media. Few of us will ever forget where we were standing the moment we heard about the passenger planes slamming into the World Trade Center towers. I was in my house, watching the morning news on television. Like most other North Americans, I spent the better part of that day glued to the television, waiting to see what might happen next.

When Jesus returns you will not have to turn to CNN to see what's happening. You will witness it for yourself. Notice what Jesus Himself said: "And then shall appear the sign of the Son of man in heaven: and then shall all the tribes of the earth mourn, and they shall see the Son of man coming in the clouds of heaven with power and great glory" (Matthew 24:30).

Here's another passage worth examining. "For as the lightning cometh out of the east, and shineth even unto the west; so shall also the coming of the Son of man be" (verse 27).

Jesus compares His return to the brilliant spectacle of lightning streaking across the sky from one horizon to another. There's a good reason He chose that language: Few people miss lightning when it flashes, and nobody's going to miss the Second Coming.

You Will Hear Jesus Coming—Not only will the Second Coming be *visible,* it will also be *audible:* "Our God shall come, and shall not keep silence: a fire shall devour before him, and it shall be very tempestuous round about him" (Psalm 50:3).

"And he shall send his angels with a great sound of a trumpet, and they shall gather together his elect from the four winds, from one end of heaven to the other" (Matthew 24:31).

Any theory that teaches that Jesus will sneak into the world to secretly steal away His people is inherently flawed. People who sneak into places typically try to avoid making a lot of noise, yet the Bible says that when Jesus returns it will be with a lot of deliberate noisemaking. Scripture describes it as the sound of trumpets and shouting.

Notice what Paul says will happen: "For the Lord himself shall descend from heaven with a shout, with the voice of the archangel, and with the trump of God: and the dead in Christ shall rise first: then we which are alive and remain shall be caught up together with them in the clouds, to meet the Lord in the air: and so shall we ever be with the Lord" (1 Thessalonians 4:16, 17).

Have you heard the expression "Loud enough to wake the dead"? I have a hunch that whoever coined that expression borrowed heavily from the writings of Paul. When Jesus returns, a trumpet blast and a mighty shout will literally awaken the dead. Without question—you'll hear Jesus come.

When Jesus Comes, Earth's History Is Finished—Perhaps one of the most dangerous byproducts of dispensationalist eschatology is the concept that after the "secret" rapture, history on Planet Earth will continue for another seven years. In other words, if you get left behind in the Second Coming, you will still have time to get your act together and start serving God.

That's a deadly misinterpretation of prophecy, and it lulls some people into inactivity and a false sense of security. Satan understands that the blessed hope of the Second Coming has long been the rallying call of Christians and a major impetus behind the spread of the gospel to the world. If he can create a sense of apathy or lethargy even among Christians, it will greatly hinder all evangelism.

The Bible is clear that humanity will have no second chance. When Jesus returns, our world's history (as we know it) will have reached its climax. "For the Son of man shall come in the glory of his Father with his angels; and then he shall reward every man according to his works" (Matthew 16:27).

Try to imagine the magnitude of this event. Jesus arrives in the "glory of his Father" with His angels. In fact, Scripture tells

us that *all* the angels will come with Jesus—billions of them.*
The history of the world has nothing to compare it with. Just
one angel was enough to knock an entire group of Roman soldiers flat on their backs! (see Matthew 28:2-4).

It will be a fitting way to end a sinful world's history. Jesus
returns in glory and sends His angels around the globe to gather
those who stand under the bloodstained banner of Calvary (see
Matthew 24:31). God will give out rewards. Notice what Paul
said about the Second Coming: "Henceforth there is laid up for
me a crown of righteousness, which the Lord, the righteous
judge, shall give me at that day: and not to me only, but unto
all them also that love his appearing" (2 Timothy 4:8).

Paul clearly places his reward in the context of Jesus' appearing. When Jesus appears all decisions will be final. We will
have no second chance to repent after Jesus returns. Notice that
when Jesus comes in glory, He will "reward every man according to his works" (Matthew 16:27). If some people remain left
behind for another seven years, during which time they could
still choose Christ, how could Jesus give "every man" his reward before that time?

Obviously He couldn't. The Bible teaches that when Jesus
returns, probation has closed. All will have decided for or
against Christ for all time. Christ will reward every man,
woman, and child for the choices they have made and the way
they have spent their lives.

Listen to the words of Jesus just before He leaves heaven to
return for us: "He that is unjust, let him be unjust still: and he
which is filthy, let him be filthy still: and he that is righteous, let
him be righteous still: and he that is holy, let him be holy still.
And, behold, I come quickly; and my reward is with me, to give
every man according as his work shall be" (Revelation 22:11, 12).

It's no wonder that the doctrine of Christ's return has become such a source of confusion. Leagues of fallen angels have
a vested interest in making the subject unclear. When Christ returns, all decisions are final. It will be too late to choose Christ.

That is why the wicked respond as they do when Jesus returns: "And the heaven departed as a scroll when it is rolled together; and every mountain and island were moved out of their

places. And the kings of the earth, and the great men, and the rich men, and the chief captains, and the mighty men, and every bondman, and every free man, hid themselves in the dens and in the rocks of the mountains; and said to the mountains and rocks, Fall on us, and hide us from the face of him that sitteth on the throne, and from the wrath of the Lamb: for the great day of his wrath is come; and who shall be able to stand?" (Revelation 6:14-17).

It is perhaps one of the most tragic scenes depicted in the Bible. The wicked panic when they finally see Jesus coming. Why? Because they know they're done for. They understand, perhaps intuitively, that it's too late to make any changes. Probation has closed. The Holy Spirit has ceased to plead with them to turn their lives over to Christ. They have chosen against God, and now they will not enjoy an eternity with Him.

Another group, however, respond quite differently when they see Jesus returning. They have chosen not to buy into the devil's deceptions but rather to bank everything on the blessed hope. They lived courageous lives, because like the first disciples, in their hearts they *knew* that the risen Jesus would return.

These faithful Christians do not beg for the rocks and mountains to fall on them. Instead, they shout with excitement: "Lo, this is our God; we have waited for him, and he will save us: this is the Lord; we have waited for him, we will be glad and rejoice in his salvation" (Isaiah 25:9).

What will *you* shout when Jesus returns?

---

* Matthew 25:31 tells us that all of the angels will come with Jesus. Revelation 5:11 lists that number as "ten thousand times ten thousand, and thousands of thousands," or well into the billions or trillions.

GLOSSARY

Amillennialism

A doctrine teaching that the expression "thousand years" of Bible prophecy is merely a figurative expression referring either to Christ's kingdom in this age or to no specific time at all.

Dispensationalism

A dividing of world history into seven ages, or "dispensations"—time periods in each of which God supposedly deals differently with humanity. This scheme regards the "church age" or Christian Era as a "parenthesis," or gap, in prophecy—as an age of pure grace between a past Jewish dispensation of law and a future one in which the Jews will again be the people of God and will rule the nations under a restoration of the Mosaic code.

Eschatology

The doctrine of the last or final things, it includes such concepts as death, resurrection, immortality, and judgment.

Exegesis

A scrutinizing or detailed analysis and interpretation or explanation of a portion of Scripture.

Futurism

A system of Bible interpretation developed by Catholic scholars at the time of the Counter-Reformation, teaching that the antichrist is a malign dictator who will appear during a tribulation period at some remote age in the future.

Hermeneutics

The science of interpretation and explanation, especially that branch of theology that defines the laws of applied exegesis.

Literalism

A theory or practice of following the letter or literal sense of interpretation, with a particular "demand" for prophetic fulfillment in absolute literalness.

Postmillennialism — The doctrine that the second coming of Jesus follows the 1,000-year period of Bible prophecy.

Posttribulationalism — A term used by dispensationalists to refer to those Christians who believe that the church will go through the tribulation.

Premillennialism — The doctrine that the Second Coming precedes the 1,000 years of Bible prophecy.

Pretribulationalism — A view holding that the "rapture," or taking up of the saints (the church) from the earth, precedes the tribulation under a yet-future antichrist.

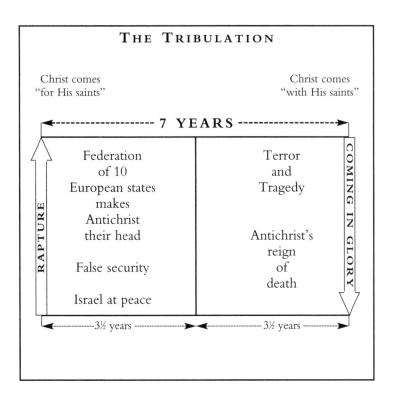

THE TRIBULATION

Christ comes "for His saints"

Christ comes "with His saints"

←-------------------- 7 YEARS -------------------→

RAPTURE

Federation of 10 European states makes Antichrist their head

False security

Israel at peace

Terror and Tragedy

Antichrist's reign of death

COMING IN GLORY

←--------------3½ years-----------------→←------------------3½ years------------→

THE "GAP"

DANIEL 2   DANIEL 7

70 WEEKS OF DANIEL 9

69 WEEKS

Babylon
605 B.C.

Medo-Persia
538 B.C.

Greece
331 B.C.

Rome
168 B.C.

THE GREAT PARENTHESIS
"the church age" some 2,000 years long

A.D.
476
1 WEEK
The Tribulation

THE DISPENSATIONS

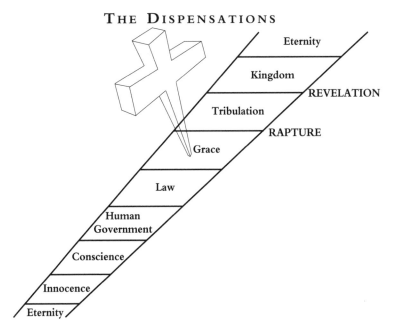

"WHAT THE PROPHETS SAW"

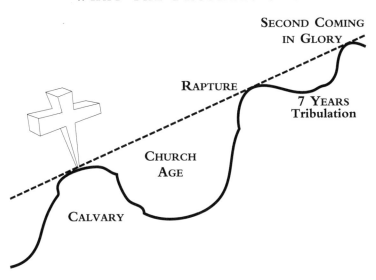

THE BIBLE MILLENNIUM

PEOPLE OF EARTH			
Believers		**Unbelievers**	
Living	Dead	Living	Dead

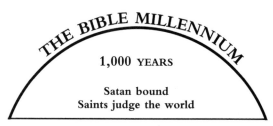

THE BIBLE MILLENNIUM

1,000 YEARS

**Satan bound
Saints judge the world**

FIRST RESURRECTION	**SECOND RESURRECTION**
Righteous dead raised	Holy City and saints descend
Righteous translated and taken to heaven	*Wicked dead* raised
Wicked destroyed by brightness of His coming	Satan loosed a season
	Fire destroys the wicked
Satan bound	Earth recreated as home of the saved